Pass **ECDL4**

Module 3: Word Processing

Using Microsoft Word 2003

P.M. Heathcote

Published by

PAYNE-GALLWAY
P U B L I S H E R S L T D

26-28 Northgate Street, Ipswich IP1 3DB
Tel: 01473 251097 Fax: 01473 232758

www.payne-gallway.co.uk

Acknowledgements

Every effort has been made to contact copyright owners of material published in this book. We would be glad to hear from unacknowledged sources at the earliest opportunity.

Cover design by Direction Advertising and Design Ltd

First Edition 2004

A catalogue entry for this book is available from the British Library.

ISBN 1 904467 31 8

Copyright © P.M. Heathcote 2004

The ECDL Trade Mark is the registered trade mark of The European Computer Driving Licence Foundation Limited in Ireland and other countries.

This ECDL Foundation approved courseware product incorporates learning reinforcement exercises. These exercises are included to help the candidate in their training for the ECDL. The exercises included in this courseware product are not ECDL certification tests and should not be construed in any way as ECDL certification tests. For information about Authorised ECDL Test Centres in different National Territories please refer to the ECDL Foundation web site at www.ecdl.com

All rights reserved

Printed in Malta by Gutenberg Press

Disclaimer

Preface

Who is this book for?

This book is suitable for anyone studying for ECDL Version 4.0 (Module 3), either at school, adult class or at home. It is suitable for complete beginners or those with some prior experience, and takes the learner step-by-step from the very basics to the point where they will feel confident using Microsoft Word to create documents and perform tasks such as formatting, copying and pasting text, inserting graphics and printing.

The approach

The approach is very much one of "learning by doing". Each module is divided into a number of chapters which correspond to one lesson. The student is guided step-by-step through a practical task at the computer, with numerous screenshots to show exactly what should be on their screen at each stage. Each individual in a class can proceed at their own pace, with little or no help from a teacher. At the end of most chapters there are exercises which provide invaluable practice. By the time a student has completed the module, every aspect of the ECDL syllabus will have been covered.

Software used

The instructions and screenshots are based on a PC running Microsoft Windows XP and Microsoft Word 2003. However, it will be relatively easy to adapt the instructions for use with other versions of Word.

Extra resources

Answers to practice exercises and other useful supporting material can be found on the publisher's web site www.payne-gallway.co.uk/ecdl.

About ECDL

The European Computer Driving Licence (ECDL) is the European-wide qualification enabling people to demonstrate their competence in computer skills. Candidates must study and pass the test for each of the seven modules listed below before they are awarded an ECDL certificate. The ECDL tests must be undertaken at an accredited test centre. For more details of ECDL tests and test centres, visit the ECDL web site www.ecdl.com.

Module 1: Concepts of Information Technology

Module 2: Using the Computer and Managing Files

Module 3: Word Processing

Module 4: Spreadsheets

Module 5: Database

Module 6: Presentation

Module 7: Information and Communication

Module 3
Word Processing

This module covers the basics of word processing. You will learn how to accomplish everyday tasks associated with creating, formatting and finishing small documents. You will learn how to:

- copy and move text within or between documents
- create standard tables
- use pictures and images within a document
- use mail merge tools
- print documents

Module 3   Table of Contents

First Steps

For this module you will be using Microsoft Word, one of many word processing packages. Word 2003 has been used in this book but you should not have any problems following the instructions if you are using a different version of Word.

For some of the exercises you will need to use files that can be downloaded from our web site. To do this:

◉   Log on to the Payne-Gallway web site **www.payne-gallway.co.uk/ecdl**.

◉   Follow the instructions to download files when you need them. Save them in a convenient folder.

You're ready to start!

Loading Word

◉   Load **Microsoft Word**. You can do this in one of two ways:

◉   *Either* double-click the **Word** icon

◉   *Or* click **Start** at the bottom left of the screen. Click on **Programs**, then click

Microsoft Office Word 2003

The opening screen

Your opening screen will look something like this:

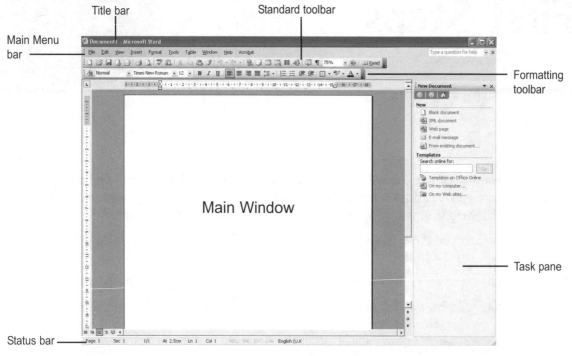

The following labels point to parts of the screen: Title bar, Standard toolbar, Main Menu bar, Formatting toolbar, Main Window, Task pane, Status bar

❶ The **Title bar** shows the name of your document, which might be, for example, a story or letter. If you have not given it a name yet, it will say **Document1** or perhaps **Document2** if this is your second document since you started **Microsoft Word** in this chapter.

❶ The **Main Menu bar** has options for you to choose from. You'll be using it when you need to edit, print or save your document.

❶ The **Standard toolbar** has a number of buttons with pictures called **icons** which are sometimes clicked instead of choosing from the main menu.

❶ The **Formatting toolbar** has icons which let you change the way your text looks – for example, making the letters bigger or smaller, bold or italic.

❶ The **Main Window** is the area of the screen in which you type.

❶ The **Status bar** shows what page you are on and how many pages there are in the document.

❶ The **Task pane** opens and closes automatically depending on what you are doing. You can close the Task pane at any time by clicking the **Close** icon (X) in its top right-hand corner.

The keyboard

Your keyboard will look like this:

Some of the keys have been labelled on the diagram:

ℹ️ The **Shift** key. As long as you hold this down, all the letters you type will be in capitals.

ℹ️ The **Caps Lock** key. If you want a whole sentence to be in capitals, you can use the **Caps Lock** key. Just press it once and release it. All the letters you type after that will be capitals. Press **Caps Lock** again when you want to stop typing capitals.

ℹ️ The **Backspace** key. This deletes the letter to the left of where the cursor is flashing. If you are typing something and press a wrong letter, pressing **Backspace** will delete it and you can then type the right letter. Very useful!

ℹ️ The **Delete** key. This deletes the letter to the right of where the cursor is flashing. It is not as useful as the **Backspace** key for correcting mistakes that you make as you are going along, but you will find it comes in useful.

ℹ️ The **Tab** key – Use this to advance the cursor to the next tab stop.

ℹ️ The **Enter** key – Use this when you want to go to a new line.

Tip:

There are two **Enter** keys on the keyboard - one marked with a bent arrow and the other marked '**Enter**'. They both do exactly the same thing. People who are typing lists of numbers find it easier to use the key near the numbers, while those using the main part of the keyboard to type text would probably prefer the one near the letters.

Creating a new document

When you start Word, a new document automatically appears on the screen. You can see in the Title bar that it is called **Document1**.

You can start to type straight away.

◐   Type the beginnings of a letter:

Dear Mrs Coates

Tip:
Use the **Shift** key, not the **Caps Lock** key, to type the upper case letters **D**, **M** and **C**.

The pointer, cursor and insertion point

As you move the mouse around, the pointer moves around the screen. The pointer looks different depending on where it is on the screen.

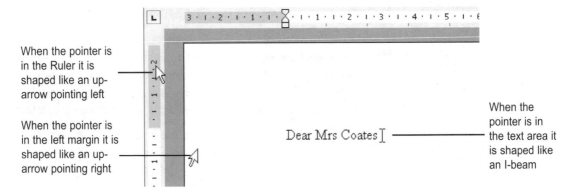

When the pointer is in the Ruler it is shaped like an up-arrow pointing left

When the pointer is in the left margin it is shaped like an up-arrow pointing right

When the pointer is in the text area it is shaped like an I-beam

If you click in different places in and around your text, the flashing vertical line (called the **cursor**) appears in different places. It marks the **insertion point** – that is, the point at which text will be inserted when you start to type.

◐   Position the pointer at the end of the line. Take care that the pointer is the **I-beam** shape – not an arrow shape – before clicking.

◐   Press **Enter** twice. (Pressing **Enter** takes you to a new line, so pressing it twice will leave one blank line between paragraphs.)

◐   Type the following sentences. (Do not press **Enter** at the end of each line.) You should leave one space after a comma (but not before) and one or two spaces after a full-stop. Decide which you prefer and then stick to it!

I am writing to invite you on a trip to Tanzania to see some of the current conservation work being sponsored by the Global Environment Association. You will be able to see first-hand the areas your money is reaching and the difference it can make.

You will notice that Word starts a new line automatically when it reaches the end of a line. You should only press **Enter** when you want to start a new paragraph.

Editing text

Now you can practise inserting and deleting text.

There are two 'editing modes' known as **Insert** and **Overtype**. The mode is controlled by pressing the **Insert** key on the keyboard. (It is just to the right of the **Backspace** key.) Try pressing this key once, and you will see that the letters **OVR** appear in the Status bar at the bottom of the screen. When you press the **Insert** key again, the letters **OVR** are greyed out, because the **Insert** key acts as a toggle.

| Page 1 | Sec 1 | 1/1 | At 2.5cm | Ln 1 | Col 4 | REC TRK EXT OVR English (U.S |

In **Overtype** mode, when you click in your text to edit it, anything that you type will replace what is already there. In **Insert** mode, anything that you type is inserted into the text.

- Make sure that you are in **Insert** mode (the words **OVR** at the bottom of the screen should be greyed out. If they are not, press the **Insert** key once.)

- Place the cursor just after the **a** of **on a trip**, click to create an insertion point and type **n interesting**. The text should now read

  I am writing to invite you on an interesting trip …

You can alter text by highlighting it and then typing the new text. A single word can be highlighted by double-clicking it. To highlight longer pieces of text, click and hold the left mouse button while you drag across the text.

- Double-click **interesting** to select it. It should appear white on a black background.

- Type the word **exciting**. This will replace the selected word.

Tip:
When text is selected you don't have to delete it before typing over it.

- Place the cursor just after the **t** of **current** and click to create an insertion point. Press the **Backspace** key several times to delete the word **current**. Insert the word **currently** after **work**.

- Now click at the end of the sentence you have typed, and press **Enter** twice.

- Finish off the letter by typing

> With best regards
>
>
> Brian Harding
> Fundraising Executive

Your letter should now look like this:

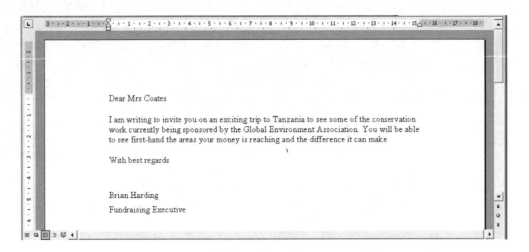

Saving your work

If you want to keep your work, so that you are able to add to it or change it at any time, you must keep it safe in a **file** on a disk. (This is called **saving a file**.)

You can save files on the **hard disk** inside the computer, or on a **floppy disk** that you can insert into the floppy disk drive and take out when you have finished saving.

○   Click **File**, **Save** on the Main Menu bar.

You'll see a screen rather like the one below. You will have different folders and subfolders from the ones shown.

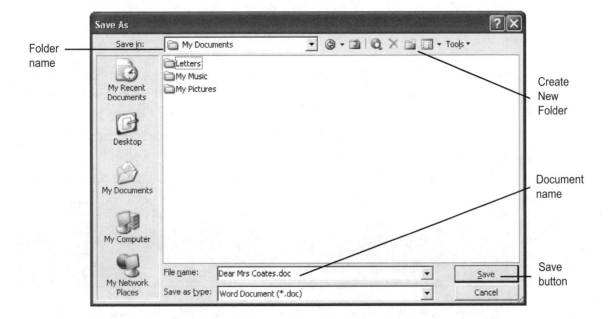

Word guesses a name for your file, which will be the first word or first few words you typed. The name appears in the **File name** box. The file name will be highlighted to show that it is selected ready for you to change it if you want to.

◐   Type a new file name. Choose a name that will remind you of what the file contains, like **TanzaniaLetter**.

Microsoft Word will add a full stop and the three letters **doc** to the name you choose. This shows that it is a document created using **Microsoft Word**.

You will be given the choice of which folder you wish to save your document in.

In the figure opposite, **Letters** is a subfolder of **My Documents**. If you want to create a subfolder in your own **My Documents** folder, click the **Create New Folder** button and then give your folder a suitable name.

To save in the **Letters** folder shown in the figure above:

◐   Double-click **Letters** to put it in the **Save in:** box.

◐   Leave the **Save as type:** box as **Word Document (*.doc)**. Before you click the **Save** button, read the next paragraph. Clicking **Save** saves your document and automatically closes the dialogue box.

Saving as another file type

By default your letter will be saved as a Word document, shown by the so-called **extension**, in this case **.doc**, at the end of the file name. If you click the down-arrow in the **Save as type:** box, you will see that you have the option of saving the file as another type.

❶   If you wanted to put this document on a web site, you would save it with the extension **.htm**.

❶   To save a document in **Rich Text Format**, select the extension **.rtf**. This is a useful format if you wish to transfer text between different word processing packages or versions without losing formatting information.

❶   To save the document as a text file with no formatting, which can be imported into another type of package, save it with the extension **.txt**.

❶   To save a document as a template (such as the customised fax template discussed in Chapter 3.4) save with the extension **.dot**.

❶   Scroll down to see other options. For example, you can save the document so that it can be read in an earlier version of Word.

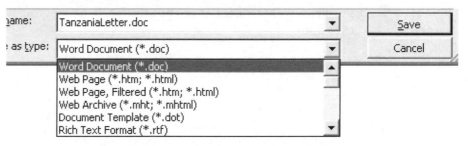

❶ You can also save a document with a software specific file extension (e.g. **.wps** for Works 2000), or in a format that can be read by a previous version of Word (e.g. Word 6.0).

◑ Now click **Save**. Close your document by selecting **File, Close** from the Main Menu bar.

Opening an existing document

You can open your document again any time to edit or print it.

◑ From the main menu select **File**.

You will see at the bottom of the menu a list of the most recently used documents.

◑ Click the file name **TanzaniaLetter**. Your document opens ready for you to work on.

◑ Now close the file again so that you can practise opening it a different way.

◑ From the menu select **File, Open**. You will see a window similar to the one below:

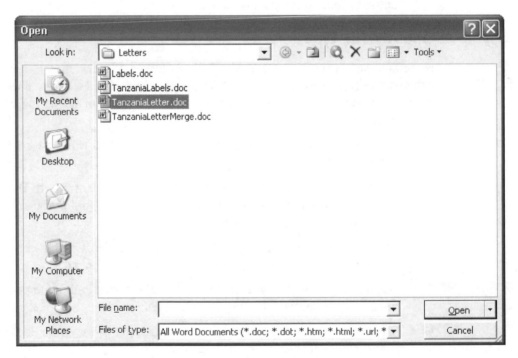

◑ Double-click **TanzaniaLetter** to open the file. Or, you can single-click it and then click **Open**.

Changing defaults and preferences

By default (i.e. unless you tell it otherwise) Word saves your documents in a folder called **My Documents** on the **C:** drive. You can change this default as well as many other preferences.

◐ From the main menu select **Tools, Options**.

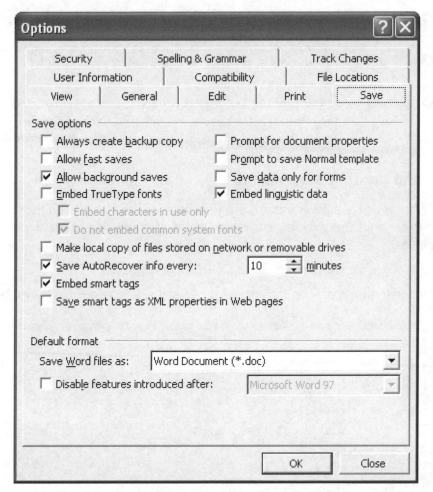

◐ Click the **File Locations** tab.

You will now be able to change the default directory for opening and saving files.

By clicking on the **Save** tab in the Options window, you can change various defaults such as how frequently your document is automatically saved.

Clicking on the **User information tab** will open a window which allows you to change the name of the author of documents you write. This name appears in a 'tip' as you hover over a file name in Windows Explorer or when opening a file.

Inserting a paragraph

You can insert the recipient's address and a date at the head of the letter. You can assume that the letter would be printed on headed stationery, so you need to leave some space at the top of the letter for this.

❍ Make sure the insertion point is at the top of the letter.

❍ Press **Enter** several times to give yourself some blank lines, and then press the **up-arrow** key to put the cursor on the new blank line.

❍ Type a name and address, followed by today's date, pressing **Enter** at the end of each line.

❍ Check your letter carefully and if all is correct, save it again by selecting **File**, **Save** from the menu. This time you won't be asked to name the file. The new version will overwrite your original letter.

Previewing and printing a document

Before you print a document it is always a good idea to look at it on the screen in **Print Preview** mode. You may spot something that needs correcting before sending it to the printer.

 ❍ Click the **Print Preview** button.

Your letter will appear on the screen exactly as it will be printed, as shown below:

Mrs R. Coates
5 Hillcrest Avenue
Cochester
Essex CR3 5RR

29 December 2002

Dear Mrs Coates

I am writing to invite you on an exciting trip to Tanzania to see some of the conservation work currently being sponsored by the Global Environment Association. You will be able to see first-hand the areas your money is reaching and the difference it can make.

With best regards

Brian Harding
Fundraising Executive

If you need to make any further corrections, press **Esc** or click the **Close** button on the **Print Preview** menu bar to return to **Print Layout** view.

○ When you have made any corrections, look at the document again in **Print Preview** mode, and then select **File**, **Print** from the menu bar. You will see the following window appear:

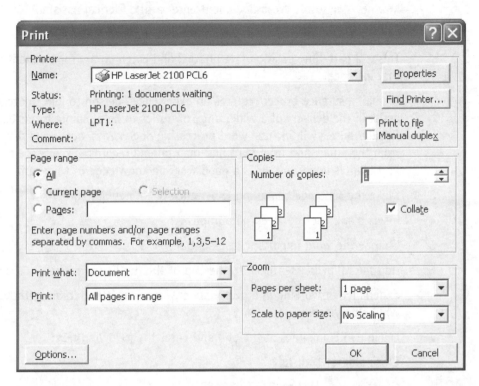

In this window you can select print options such as: print entire document, specified pages, specified number of copies, print a document to file, switch collation on or off.

You can also select which printer to send the output to. If you have no printer available, you can click the **Print to File** checkbox to send a Print File to, say, a floppy disk from where it can be printed later, perhaps on another computer attached to a printer.

○ Make sure that your computer is connected to a printer, that the printer is turned on and that paper is loaded.

○ Click **OK** to print the document.

○ If all is well, select **File**, **Close** from the menu bar to close the document.

Closing Microsoft Word

There are several ways of closing **Word**.

❶ Click the **X** in the top right-hand corner.

❶ Click the **Word** icon in the top left-hand corner and from the dropdown menu select **Close**.

❶ From the **File** menu select **Exit**.

Exercise

You are preparing an advertisement for the local newspaper.

1. In a new Microsoft Word document enter a title **Clerical Assistant**.

2. Leave a blank line and then enter the following information:

    This is a part-time position (18.5 hours) and is temporary for six months in the first instance.

    A small insurance broker requires an experienced person to join the team and assist in the delivery of a wide range of duties to help maintain this busy office. Regular duties will include word processing documents; dealing with queries from the public and from staff and maintaining records. Experience of working in a team is important, as is a good working knowledge of Microsoft Office.

3. Make the sentence beginning **Experience of...** a new paragraph.

4. Insert blank lines between paragraphs.

5. Change the word **important** to **essential**.

6. Add the following sentence to the end of the third paragraph:

    Experience of working in a personnel environment is preferable, although training will be provided.

7. Leave two blank lines at the end and enter the following text:

    Closing date: 18th July

    Contact: Jane Hall on 01578 23455.

8. Delete the words **in the first instance** in the first paragraph.

9. Save the document as **Job advert**.

Clerical Assistant

This is a part-time position (18.5 hours) and is temporary for six months.

A small insurance broker requires an experienced person to join the team and assist in the delivery of a wide range of duties to help maintain this busy office. Regular duties will include word processing documents; dealing with queries from the public and from staff and maintaining records.

Experience of working in a team is essential, as is a good working knowledge of Microsoft Office. Experience of working in a personnel environment is preferable, although training will be provided.

Closing date: 18th July
Contact: Jane Hall on 01578 23455

Formatting

In this chapter you will learn to improve the appearance of a document by formatting it.

The document that you will format may be downloaded from the web site **www.payne-gallway.co.uk/ecdl**. (See Page 3-3 for instructions how to do this.) It is called **Itinerary.doc**. You should save the document in a suitable folder.

Alternatively, you can type it yourself. The text is given below. You are to imagine that you work for an Environmental organisation called the Global Environment Association (GEA). You are preparing an itinerary for a visit to Tanzania of a group of Association members.

Itinerary
Day 1
Depart London Heathrow on British Airways flight
Day 2
Arrive at Dar es Salaam Airport. Our representative will meet and transfer the group to the hotel. The morning will be at leisure to rest after the overnight flight. After lunch our representative will meet and escort you to the GEA offices. The Country Representative, Dr David Moshi, will give a presentation and brief you on the GEA projects in Tanzania.
Day 3
After breakfast your guide will meet you for the transfer to Mikumi Kiboga Camp.
Dinner and Overnight – Mikumi Kiboga Camp
Day 4
You will be met and escorted for an early morning game drive through the Mikumi Park. Return to your accommodation for breakfast.
Following breakfast your guide will escort you on the transfer to Udzungwa Mountain National Park. Followed by an accompanied late afternoon walk in the forest
Day 5
The day includes trekking and sightseeing in the area.
After breakfast your guide will escort the group on a leisurely walk to Sanje Falls, with a chance to take a refreshing swim in the falls. A picnic lunch will be provided.

Saving with another name

○ Open **Word** if it is not already open.

○ If you have saved the downloaded document **Itinerary.doc** in your own folder, click **File**, **Open** and open the document now.

○ If you have not downloaded and saved the document, you can either do so now, or type it in as shown on the previous page.

When you click the **Save** icon or use the **Save** command from the **File** menu, your document will automatically be saved using the same file name as the one that you have previously used when saving it. If you want to keep the original copy safe and save a second version of the file, you should use the **File**, **Save As**. command, which allows you to save the document using a different name to the same or a new folder.

○ From the menu bar select **File**, **Save As** to save the document as **NewItinerary.doc**.

Fonts

Font is an alternative word for **typeface**. Both words describe the actual shape of the letters that appear on the screen when you are typing. Fonts have different names like **Times New Roman**, **Arial**, and **Comic Sans MS**.

Types of font

There are two basic types of font, called **Serif** and **Sans Serif**. A serif is the little tail at the top and bottom of each letter.

Serifs

This is written in a Serif font called Times New Roman

This is written in a Sans Serif font called Arial

Taken from the French for '**without Serif**', **Sans Serif** fonts are very clear and are used in places where text needs to be clear and easy to read, such as road signs and textbooks.

Serif fonts are more often used for large amounts of text that will be read quickly, such as in newspapers or books. The serifs 'lead your eye' from one word to the next.

You should not use too many different fonts on a page – it can end up looking a mess.

Font sizes

Font sizes are measured in **points**. 6 point is about the smallest font you can read without the aid of a magnifying glass.

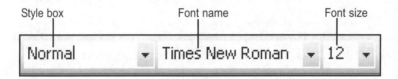

This is 6 point Times New Roman

This is 12 point Times New Roman

This is 24 point Times New Roman

Applying an existing style to a word, line or paragraph

Look at the formatting toolbar. The name and size of the default font are shown in the Style box - this is the font that **Microsoft Word** will choose for you automatically, before you change it to whatever you wish.

Style box   Font name   Font size

| Normal ▾ | Times New Roman ▾ | 12 ▾ |

You can use the Style box to apply different built-in styles to different parts of a document.

- ◉ Click the word **Itinerary**.
- ◉ Click the down-arrow in the **Style** box.
- ◉ Click the **Heading 1** style. The style of the heading will change.
- ◉ Now select the second line, **Day 1**. Click the down-arrow in the **Style** box and select the **Heading 2** style.
- ◉ Select the next paragraph and change the style to **Normal**.

Changing font and font size

We will start by changing the font and size of the heading. To change the character formatting of a single word, it is not necessary to select the whole word. It is sufficient to click anywhere in the word.

- ◉ Click in the title **Itinerary**.
- ◉ On the Formatting toolbar, click the down-arrow beside the Font box and change the font to **Arial** if it is not already in this font.
- ◉ Click the down-arrow beside the **Font Size** box and select Font Size **24**.

| Arial ▾ | 24 ▾ |

Text alignment and emboldening

You can centre the heading and make it bold, using buttons on the Formatting toolbar.

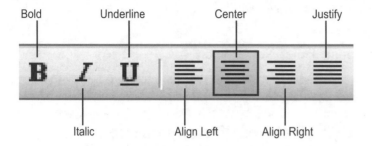

- ◉   With the cursor still somewhere in the heading, click the **Center** button. It will look pressed in when **selected** – as in the picture above.
- ◉   Click the **Bold** button to make the heading bold. Now make it underlined and italic as well.

The text under the heading is currently **left-justified**. This means that it is all lined up against the left-hand margin, and the text does not make a straight edge against the right-hand margin. You can make it do so by **justifying** the text.

- ◉   Select all the text except the title by dragging the mouse across it with the left button held down.
- ◉   Click the **Justify** button.

You can experiment with the other alignment buttons to see what the text looks like when it is centred or right-aligned.

The Undo and Redo commands

You can use the **Undo** button to undo the last action. Clicking **Undo** 3 times, for example, will undo the last 3 actions.

Click the **Redo** button to redo the last action that you undid.

Undo ———  ——— Redo

Return to justified text when you are satisfied you know what each of these buttons does.

> **Tip:**
> If you are unsure as to what any toolbar button does, simply move the pointer over it and a tip will appear informing you of its function.

Setting text colours

 To change the colour of text, you must first select the text and then click the **Font Color** button.

○ Select the title **Itinerary** and click the down-arrow next to the **Font Color** button.

○ Select the red colour.

○ Click in the left margin beside **Day 1** to select the line.

○ With the heading selected, click the **Font Color** button and select blue from the colour palette which appears.

Now you can make the other headings for Day 2, Day 3 etc the same blue. To do this we will practise using the **Repeat** command.

○ Select the heading **Day 2**.

○ From the **Edit** menu select **Repeat Font Color**.

○ Do this again for each of the other **Day** headings.

Applying case changes and other formats

You can apply formatting or case changes (e.g. make all letters uppercase) to any selected text using the **Format** command from the menu bar.

Suppose you wanted to change the case of the words **Day 1**.

○ Select the text **Day 1**.

○ From the **Format** menu select **Change Case**.

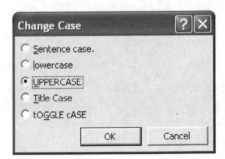

○ In the Change Case dialogue box, click the case you want to apply to the text. Try selecting the option **UPPERCASE** and click **OK**.

○ It looked better in Sentence case, so click the **Undo** button.

Now suppose you want to give the heading **Itinerary** a double underline.

○ Select the word **Itinerary**.

○   From the **Format** menu select **Font**.

○   In the **Underline Style** box choose a double underline. Click **OK**.

○   You can either leave this format or Undo it by clicking the **Undo** button.

Note:

There are options in this window for applying all kinds of formatting such as **bold**, **italic**, **underline**, **superscript**, **subscript**, **small caps**, **all caps** to text. Try out these effects so that you know what they all do.

Text superscript   Text subscript

THIS IS TEXT IN SMALL CAPS... and THIS IS TEXT IN ALL CAPS

○   Change the case of the heading **Itinerary** to **All caps**.

Changing line spacing

The document looks rather cramped and needs to be spaced out. One way of spacing out the text would be to insert a blank line between paragraphs.

○   Insert a blank line under the title **Itinerary** by clicking at the end of the line and pressing **Enter**.

You can double-space all the text. This is very useful when you are creating a draft of a document which will be checked and edited by someone else, as it allows space for corrections to be made by hand on the printed document. We'll try it now.

○   Select all the text under the title.

○   From the **Format** menu, select **Paragraph**. The following window appears:

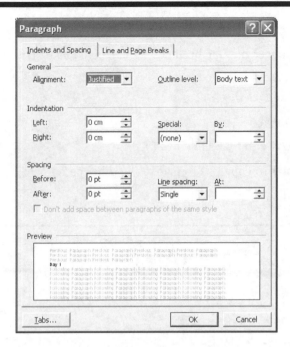

○ In the **Line Spacing** box, select **Double**. Click **OK**.

○ Examine the effect on the text. It is not quite what we want here, so click the **Undo** button to restore it to how it was.

We will try an alternative, which is to put some space before each of the 'Day' headings.

○ Select the heading **Day 1**. Then select **Format, Paragraph** again.

○ In **Spacing, Before** click the up-arrow to select **6 pt** and click **OK**.

○ Make this heading **Bold** and **Italic**.

Copying a format

You can now copy this format to other paragraphs using the **Format Painter**. To use this tool once, you select the text whose format you wish to copy, and then you select the text you want to copy the format onto. Try it like this:

 ○ With **Day 1** selected, click the **Format Painter** button once.

○ Select the heading **Day 2**. Both the character formatting (Italic) and paragraph format (6pt spacing) is copied to **Day 2**.

To copy the same format to several different bits of text, you must first select the text whose format you wish to copy, then double-click the format painter. Then you can select as many bits of text as you like. Try it now:

○ With either **Day 1** or **Day 2** selected, double-click the **Format Painter** button.

○ Select **Day 3**, **Day 4** and **Day 5** in turn to change the formatting of these lines. Then click the **Format Painter** button again to turn it off.

Indenting paragraphs

We can indent all the text under the Day headings to make the headings stand out more.

- ❂ Select the paragraph under **Day 1**.
- ❂ Select **Format, Paragraph**.
- ❂ Under **Indentation, Left** enter **0.5 cm**. Click **OK**.
- ❂ Use the **Format Painter** to copy this format to the other paragraphs.

Your text should now look like this:

ITINERARY

Day 1

Depart London Heathrow on British Airways flight

Day 2

Arrive at Dar es Salaam Airport. Our representative will meet and transfer the group to the hotel. The morning will be at leisure to rest after the overnight flight. After lunch our representative will meet and escort you to the GEA offices. The Country Representative, Dr David Moshi, will give a presentation and brief you on the GEA projects in Tanzania.

Day 3

After breakfast your guide will meet you for the transfer to Mikumi Kiboga Camp.
Dinner and Overnight – Mikumi Kiboga Camp

Day 4

You will be met and escorted for an early morning game drive through the Mikumi Park.
Return to your accommodation for breakfast.
Following breakfast your guide will escort you on the transfer to Udzungwa Mountain National Park. Followed by an accompanied late afternoon walk in the forest.

Day 5

The day includes trekking and sightseeing in the area.
After breakfast your guide will escort the group on a leisurely walk to Sanje Falls, with a chance to take a refreshing swim in the falls. A picnic lunch will be provided.

- ❂ Save and close your document.
- ❂ If you are finished for now, exit **Word**.

Exercise

In this exercise you will format the job advertisement you created in the exercise at the end of Chapter 3.1.

1. Open the file **Job advert.doc**. Save the file as **Job advert1.doc**.
2. Format the heading **Clerical Assistant** to size 18, Times New Roman, bold.
3. Now format the heading dark blue and double-underlined.
4. Delete the blank lines between paragraphs.
5. Insert spacing of 6pt before the first four paragraphs.
6. Insert the following text in on a line beneath the main heading:

    Ipswich £12k–£13.5k pro rata
7. Format this text Times New Roman, bold, size 12, dark blue and right-aligned.
8. Format the word **essential** in the third paragraph italic and bold.
9. Insert a superscript number **1** after the word **hours** in the first sentence.
10. Insert the following text on a new line at the end of the advert.

    [1]hours per week
11. Finally indent all paragraphs by 1cm on the left and 2cm on the right.
12. Save your work. It should look something like this:

Clerical Assistant

Ipswich £12k-£13.5k pro rata

This is a part-time position (18.5 hours[1]) and is temporary for six months.

A small insurance broker requires an experienced person to join the team and assist in the delivery of a wide range of duties to help maintain this busy office. Regular duties will include word processing documents; dealing with queries from the public and from staff and maintaining records.

Experience of working in a team is ***essential***, as is a good working knowledge of Microsoft Office. Experience of working in a personnel environment is preferable, although training will be provided.

Closing date: 18th July
Contact: Jane Hall on 01578 23455
[1]hours per week

Basic Operations

In this chapter you will be learning how to perform basic operations such as selecting, copying and pasting text. You will also learn how to display or hide toolbars, and how to select print options.

> ● Load **Word**. A new blank document should appear on your screen. If you already have Word running, you can click the **New Blank Document** button to start a new document.

Type the first five lines of the first verse from **Old MacDonald**. Remember to press **Enter** at the end of each line.

Old MacDonald

Old MacDonald had a farm, E-I-E-I-O
And on his farm he had a cow, E-I-E-I-O
With a "moo-moo" here and a "moo-moo" there
Here a "moo" there a "moo"
Everywhere a "moo-moo"

Tip:
Use the double-quote marks above the 2 on the keyboard. "Straight quotes" will be replaced with "smart quotes" (i.e. opening and closing quotes) if the options are set to do this under **Tools**, **AutoCorrect Options**, **AutoFormat**.

Selecting text

There are many different ways of selecting text. It is well worth getting to know them. You have already practised selecting text by holding down the left mouse button and dragging across the text. This method applies to any amount of text, from a single character to a whole document, but some quicker ways are described as follows.

When selected, black text shows up white on a black background.

To select a word:

Double-click anywhere in the word.

To select one or more lines:

Click in the left margin beside the line to select a line. Drag down the left margin to select several lines.

To select a sentence:

Hold down **Crtl** and then click anywhere in the sentence.

To select a paragraph:

Triple-click anywhere in the paragraph.

To select an entire document:

From the **Edit** menu choose **Select All**. Or, you can use the shortcut key combination **Ctrl-A**.

To select a large block of text:

Click the mouse at the beginning of the text you want to select. Then scroll to the end of the text and hold down **Shift** while you click again.

To select non-adjacent text:

Select the first bit of text, then hold down **Ctrl** while you select another piece of text.

> **Tip:**
>
> If you want to apply a format such as **Bold** to a word, you do not have to select it first. Just click anywhere in the word and then click the **Bold** button.

You can try out some of these techniques on the text you have just typed:

- ◗ Select all the text and change the font to **Comic Sans MS, Bold**, size **13.5**.
- ◗ Select the heading and make it size **18**.
- ◗ Select both the occurrences of **E-I-E-I-O**. Then make this text blue.

Copying text

The last line of the verse is a repetition of the first line.

You are going to use the **Copy** and **Paste** buttons to save yourself the trouble of having to write out the same line again.

- ◗ Select the line **Old MacDonald had a farm, E-I-E-I-O** by clicking in the left-hand margin next to the line.
- ◗ Click the **Copy** button on the **Standard toolbar**.
- ◗ Press **Enter** after the last line.
- ◗ Click at the beginning of the new blank line.
- ◗ Click the **Paste** button.

The line will be copied into the text.

Tip:
You will see an icon which looks like the **Paste** button appearing under your text. This is called a **smart tag**. It allows you to change the formatting of the text you have copied.

- Now type in the first five lines of the next two verses, leaving a blank line between each verse.

 - Use the **Format Painter** to copy the formatting - make each E-I-E-I-O blue.

Old MacDonald had a farm, E-I-E-I-O
And on his farm he had a horse, E-I-E-I-O
With a "neigh, neigh" here and a "neigh, neigh" there
Here a "neigh" there a "neigh"
Everywhere a "neigh, neigh"

Old MacDonald had a farm, E-I-E-I-O
And on his farm he had a pig, E-I-E-I-O
With a (snort) here and a (snort) there
Here a (snort) there a (snort)
Everywhere a (snort)

Cutting and pasting

Suppose we've made a mistake and Old MacDonald had a pig *before* he had a horse!

We can move the third verse back to become the second verse using the **Cut** button.

- Select the verse you have just typed (about the pig) by clicking in the margin to its left and dragging down.

 - Click on the **Cut** button on the Standard toolbar. The selected text will disappear, but it is not lost completely: It is being stored for you.

 - Now click immediately before the first line in the second verse (about the horse) and click the **Paste** button. The verse is now pasted from the clipboard into the text exactly where you want it.

- Press **Enter** after your pasted verse if you need to insert another blank line.

Cutting and pasting is very useful when you are writing your own text and want to move things around.

You have been using buttons from the Standard toolbar to **Cut**, **Copy** and **Paste**. However, if you prefer, you can use these other ways:

1.   Click **Edit**, followed by **Cut**, **Copy** or **Paste** from the **Main Menu** bar.

2.   Use the keyboard: for **Cut**, press **Ctrl-X**, for copy, press **Ctrl-C**, for **Paste**, press **Ctrl-V** (i.e. Keep **Ctrl** pressed down while you press the letter on the keyboard).

◐ Now use the **Copy** and **Paste** buttons again to duplicate the parts of the rhyme that repeat (i.e. lines 3-5 from each verse and the last line). The completed rhyme should look something like this:

Old MacDonald

Old MacDonald had a farm, E-I-E-I-O
And on his farm he had a cow, E-I-E-I-O
With a "moo-moo" here and a "moo-moo" there
Here a "moo" there a "moo"
Everywhere a "moo-moo"
Old MacDonald had a farm, E-I-E-I-O

Old MacDonald had a farm, E-I-E-I-O
And on his farm he had a pig, E-I-E-I-O
With a (snort) here and a (snort) there
Here a (snort) there a (snort)
Everywhere a (snort)
With a "moo-moo" here and a "moo-moo" there
Here a "moo" there a "moo"
Everywhere a "moo-moo"
Old MacDonald had a farm, E-I-E-I-O

Old MacDonald had a farm, E-I-E-I-O
And on his farm he had a horse, E-I-E-I-O
With a "neigh, neigh" here and a "neigh, neigh" there
Here a "neigh" there a "neigh"
Everywhere a "neigh, neigh"
With a (snort) here and a (snort) there
Here a (snort) there a (snort)
Everywhere a (snort)
With a "moo-moo" here and a "moo-moo" there
Here a "moo" there a "moo"
Everywhere a "moo-moo"
Old MacDonald had a farm, E-I-E-I-O

Finding and replacing text

Suppose that after completing your lyrics, you decide that you would prefer the pig in the rhyme to **grunt** rather than **snort**.

As you can see this word appears many times and you need a quick way of changing each occurrence.

◐ Click at the start of the first line.

○ From the Main Menu bar, select **Edit** then **Replace** (or press **Ctrl-H** on the keyboard).

You will see a dialogue box and you can type the word or phrase you want to replace, and the word or phrase to replace it with.

You can get the computer to replace all occurrences, or search for them one at a time so that you can decide whether or not to replace each one. In this case you want them all replaced.

○ Click the button marked **Replace All**. Word tells you how many words have been replaced.

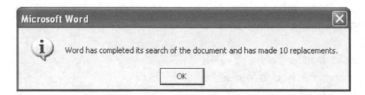

○ Save your document as **Old Macdonald.doc**.

Note that if you simply want to find a specific word or phrase you should select **Edit**, **Find** from the Main Menu bar.

Displaying and hiding built-in toolbars

When you open **Word**, the Standard toolbar and the Formatting toolbar should be displayed by default. There are many other toolbars which you may need from time to time. And if for some reason the Standard toolbar or Formatting toolbar is not displayed, you need to know how to get them back!

○ From the **View** menu on the menu bar, select **Toolbars**.

A list of toolbars appears.

Notice that the toolbars that are ticked are the ones that are visible on your screen. If you click them to deselect them, they will no longer be displayed.

○ If the Drawing toolbar is not ticked, select it now.

The Drawing toolbar usually appears at the bottom of the screen.

This toolbar is used to draw lines, shapes and text boxes. We will draw a line between each verse.

Drawing a horizontal line

◗   Select the **Line** tool from the Drawing toolbar.

◗   Keep your finger on the **Shift** key while you draw a line between the first and second verse. You can drag it to position it correctly.

Tip:
Keeping your finger on **Shift** while you draw a line ensures that it will be horizontal.

◗   With the line still selected, click the **Line Style** button, and set a different line style.

◗   Now comes the clever bit! Press both **Shift** and **Ctrl** and keep them pressed down while you drag the line down to between the second and third verses. Then drag again to the end of the third verse.

Old MacDonald

Old MacDonald had a farm, E-I-E-I-O
And on his farm he had a cow, E-I-E-I-O
With a "moo-moo" here and a "moo-moo" there
Here a "moo" there a "moo"
Everywhere a "moo-moo"
Old MacDonald had a farm, E-I-E-I-O

Old MacDonald had a farm, E-I-E-I-O
And on his farm he had a pig, E-I-E-I-O
With a (grunt) here and a (grunt) there
Here a (grunt) there a (grunt)
Everywhere a (grunt)
With a "moo-moo" here and a "moo-moo" there
Here a "moo" there a "moo"
Everywhere a "moo-moo"
Old MacDonald had a farm, E-I-E-I-O

Old MacDonald had a farm, E-I-E-I-O
And on his farm he had a horse, E-I-E-I-O
With a "neigh, neigh" here and a "neigh, neigh" there
Here a "neigh" there a "neigh"
Everywhere a "neigh, neigh"
With a (grunt) here and a (grunt) there
Here a (grunt) there a (grunt)
Everywhere a (grunt)
With a "moo-moo" here and a "moo-moo" there
Here a "moo" there a "moo"
Everywhere a "moo-moo"
Old MacDonald had a farm, E-I-E-I-O

You should have three identical lines. Keeping a finger on **Ctrl** copies, rather than moves, an object. Keeping a finger on **Shift** means that the object can only move vertically while you drag down, which ensures that all the lines will be perfectly lined up.

Spell-checking

You should always spell-check a document before you print it. When you type a document, any words that Word does not recognise are underlined with a red squiggle.

It will also underline in red repeated words, so if for example you write '**I went to the the cinema**', the second occurrence of '**the**' will be underlined in red.

Parts of the text that Word thinks are not grammatical will be underlined in green, though you may disagree. You will also see a green wavy line if you leave two spaces rather than one between words.

Word cannot know when you have simply typed the wrong word, like "widow" instead of "window" or "their" instead of "there", so you still need to check your own spelling carefully even if nothing is underlined in red.

To try out the spell-checker, put some errors in Old Macdonald.

○ Delete the **h** in **everywhere** in the first verse. Replace every other occurrence of **everywhere** with this misspelt word.

○ Replace the first occurrence of **there** with **their**.

 ○ Now position the pointer at the start of the document and click the **Spelling and Grammar** button.

A window opens offering you suggestions for the first misspelling:

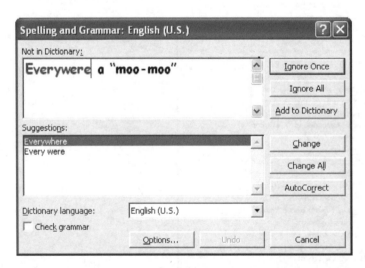

○ You can accept the first suggestion, which looks correct, and change every occurrence. Click **Change All**.

Word does not find the misspelling of **there**. You will have to correct that one yourself.

○ Put one more misspelling in so that you can try out the shortcut menu. Change **Old** to **Oold**.

○ As soon as you click away from the word it will be underlined in red. Right-click the word and the shortcut menu appears.

○ Click the correct spelling and the word will be corrected.

If Word does not recognise a word that you know is correctly spelt, you can add it to the dictionary. For example, the word 'misspelt' is not recognised, but it is correctly spelt so you could click **Add to Dictionary**. Alternatively, if you have a word or an abbreviation that you want to use frequently in your current document, but you do not want to add it to the dictionary, you can click **Ignore All**. The word will only be ignored in the current document.

○ Save your document.

Proofreading your document

Before you print a document you should proofread it carefully. Check the spelling and grammar and then check for errors of layout and presentation, including appropriate margins, font sizes and formats.

Previewing your document

When you have carefully checked your document you should preview it before printing it. This will show you what the page will look like when it is printed.

○ Click the **Print Preview** button on the Standard toolbar.

○ Click the **Close Preview** button to return to Print Layout view and make any corrections that are needed before you print.

○ Close your document, saving again if you have made any changes.

○ Close **Word**.

Exercise

You have been asked to produce a report for a school football match.

1.   Enter the following text into a new word processing document. Use Arial, size 11 font.

Year 7 Football Barksfield v Holdbrook, Thursday 25 February

There was plenty of action in both halves during the first period of the game, with both goalies having plenty to do. The finest save of the match came from the brilliant Jamie Dereham in the Barksfield goal. As a shot came in from the edge of the area, flying into the bottom corner of the net, Jamie leapt up to deftly punch it away. Unfortunately a Holdbrook forward picked up the rebound and before Jamie was back on his feet the opposition had netted their first. The score remained the same until half time.

In the second half Barksfield rallied well with both Doug Glere and Chris Holmes creating some good runs and direct passes to feet. The visitors won a corner which was fired onto the head of a Holdbrook player, but the shot was superbly cleared off the line by Alex Beardshaw. Holdbrook maintained the pressure and won another corner. This time Barksfield were not so lucky and a superb goal was scored directly from the corner flag. This was a closely fought game between two well-matched sides. Full time score: Barksfield 0 Holdbrook 2.

2.   Run the spell-checker and correct any typing errors.

3.   Make the heading Arial, size 14 and bold.

4.   Cut the complete sentence **This was a closely fought...** in the last paragraph and paste it at the beginning of the first paragraph.

5.   The visiting team is called **Holdbroom**, not **Holdbrook**. Use the Find and Replace feature to replace all occurrences of the word **Holdbrook** with **Holdbroom**.

6.   This may be used as an article in the school newsletter. As such it will require a horizontal line beneath the article. Display the Drawing toolbar and draw a short thick line, centred beneath the text.

7.   Proof read the document before you save it.

8.   Check the document in Print Preview before printing it.

Working with Many Documents

In this chapter you will be doing some more work on the travel itinerary that you started in Chapter 3.2.

Imagine that you want to write some more information about the places that the tourists will visit. However, you want to check your facts first by sending a fax to someone in Tanzania to cast an eye over.

Using a template

Word has many different **templates** which are used for different types of document such as a letter, fax, memo, formal report or web page. In fact, every time you open a new document you are using a template, probably without realising it.

▶ Load **Word**. From the **File** menu select **New**.

The Task pane appears on the right of the screen, if it is not already visible.

▶ In Office 2003, click on **On my computer** under **Templates**. In Office XP, in the **New from Template** list at the bottom of the Task pane, select **General Templates**.

The following screen will be displayed:

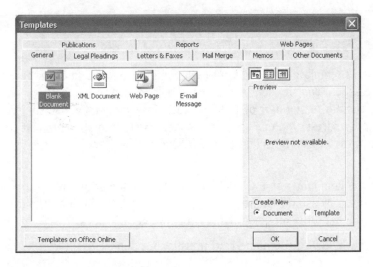

Normally you would select **Blank Document**. This is the default template that Word uses when you simply click the **New Blank Document** icon.

This time, however, we are going to select a template that will be suitable for writing a fax.

◗   Click the **Letters & Faxes** tab. You will see that there are several different templates for you to choose from.

◗   Select the **Professional Fax** template, and click **OK**.

You will see the following document appear:

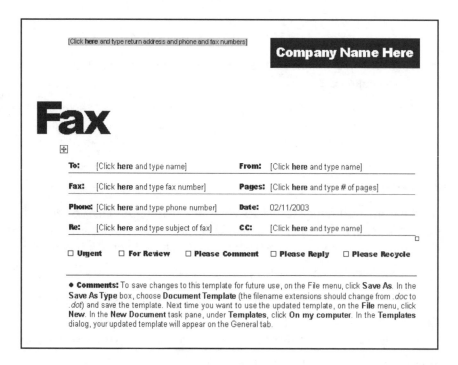

Tip:

cc stands for **carbon copy**. Only use this if you are sending a copy of the fax to a second person.

You can use this template to insert your own company name and other details including message. Read the comments at the bottom of the fax. You will see that if you want to customise any part of this template, for example by inserting a company logo and return address, you can save your customised template. The next time you want to use it, the name you select (e.g. **GEAFaxForm**) will appear in the list of templates.

◗   Fill in the company name **Global Environment Association** and return address (make it up or use the address shown on Page 3-36). Fill in all the other items above the main fax message. Type **1** for Number of Pages.

◗   Save your fax with the name **FaxTanzania**, but don't close it yet.

○ Highlight the bulleted paragraph beginning **Comments:** and in its place type the text:

> Henry:
> Could you please check these paragraphs and make sure I have got all the facts right?

○ Under this text type the following paragraphs:

> Dar es Salaam is the largest city in Tanzania with an estimated 3.0 million people. It is the gateway to Zanzibar, a 75-minute ferry ride away and a starting point to the Northern and Southern safari circuit.
>
> Mikumi National Park covers an area of 3230 sq km and is the third largest park in Tanzania. It is one of the most popular parks in Tanzania and is an important centre for education, where students go to study ecology and conservation. It contains a wide range of wildlife.

Using styles

There are several different styles of text in this document.

○ Click on the line which contains the name and address. In the formatting toolbar you will see the name of the style that is being used displayed in the **Style** box.

Style name

The Style name is **Return Address**, and the font is **Arial, 8pt, left-justified**.

○ Click in other parts of the Fax document and note the different style names. You should find **Company Name**, **Document Label**, **Message Header**, **Emphasis** and **Body Text**.

When you deleted the **Comment** in the body of the fax and typed your own message, it may have appeared in the **Emphasis** style, which was the style of the word **Comment**.

You can change this style to **Body Text** as follows:

○ Select the message text by dragging down the left margin.

○ Click the down-arrow in the **Style** box to display a list of all available styles.

○ Click **Body Text** and press **Enter**.

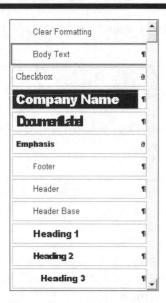

● Now press **Enter** at the end of the message to go to a new line. This time, we will apply a new style before typing anything.

● Click the down-arrow in the **Style** box to display a list of all available styles.

● Click **Emphasis** and press **Enter**.

● Type **Yours, Brian**.

● Save this document (**FaxTanzania.doc**) and close it.

Copying text between documents

Now suppose that the content of the fax message has been confirmed by Henry and you are ready to insert it into your travel itinerary.

You are going to copy the text from the document **FaxTanzania.doc** into the itinerary document.

- ◗ Open the document **NewItinerary.doc** that you created in Chapter 3.2.

- ◗ Open **FaxTanzania.doc** by clicking its icon in the Task bar.

- ◗ Select the paragraph about Dar-es-Salaam and copy it to the clipboard by pressing **Ctrl-C**.

- ◗ Click the icon for **NewItinerary.doc** to open it.

- ◗ At the end of the paragraph under **Day 2**, (just before **Day 3**), press **Enter** to insert a new paragraph.

- ◗ Press **Ctrl-V** to insert the text that you just copied.

 ◗ If it is in a different font, use the **Format Painter** to make it look the same as the rest of the text, as described in the paragraph 'Copying a Format' in Chapter 3.2.

- ◗ Indent the new paragraph 0.5cm as described at the end of Chapter 3.2.

 ◗ Similarly, insert the paragraph about Mikumi National Park under Day 3. This time, format it by selecting **Match Destination Formatting** from the **smart tag** which appeared when you pasted the paragraph.

- ◗ Delete any extra blank lines at the end of the new paragraphs by clicking on the blank line and pressing **Backspace**.

Deleting text

 To delete text, first select it and then select **Cut** from the **Edit** menu. Alternatively, click the **Delete** key on the keyboard or click the **Cut** button.

Moving text between open documents

 To move text between open documents, you can first delete it from the original document by one of the methods described above. Then click in the second document where you want the text to appear, and select Paste from the **Edit** menu, click the **Paste** button or press **Ctrl-V**.

Inserting special symbols

We will put an aeroplane symbol before and after the sentence 'Depart London Heathrow on British Airways flight'.

▶   Click at the start of the sentence.

▶   From the **Insert** menu select **Symbol**.

▶   In the **Symbol** window select the font **Wingdings**.

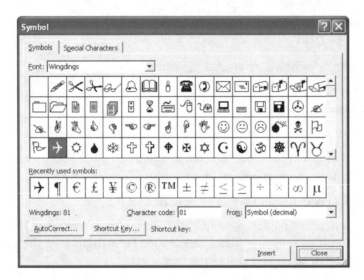

▶   Find the aeroplane symbol and click **Insert** and then **Close**.

▶   Now insert a second aeroplane symbol at the end of the sentence.

You can also insert special characters such as ©,®, etc into a document. To do this click the **Special Characters** tab in the Symbol window shown above. The following screen appears:

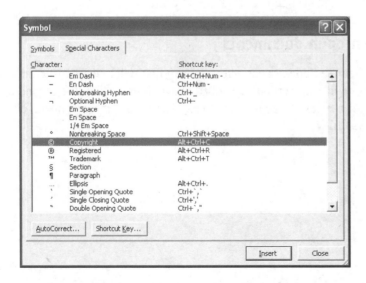

You don't need any of these characters in this document. Your itinerary should look like this:

ITINERARY

Day 1
✈ Depart London Heathrow on British Airways flight ✈

Day 2
Arrive at Dar es Salaam Airport. Our representative will meet and transfer the group to the hotel. The morning will be at leisure to rest after the overnight flight. After lunch our representative will meet and escort you to the GEA offices. The Country Representative, Dr David Moshi, will give a presentation and brief you on the GEA projects in Tanzania.
Dar es Salaam is the largest city in Tanzania with an estimated 3.0 million people. It is the gateway to Zanzibar, a 75-minute ferry ride away and a starting point to the Northern and Southern safari circuit.

Day 3
After breakfast your guide will meet you for the transfer to Mikumi Kiboga Camp.
Dinner and Overnight – Mikumi Kiboga Camp
Mikumi National Park covers an area of 3230 sq km and is the third largest park in Tanzania. It is one of the most popular parks in Tanzania and is an important centre for education, where students go to study ecology and conservation. It contains a wide range of wildlife.

Day 4
You will be met and escorted for an early morning game drive through the Mikumi Park.
Return to your accommodation for breakfast.
Following breakfast your guide will escort you on the transfer to Udzungwa Mountain National Park. Followed by an accompanied late afternoon walk in the forest.

Day 5
The day includes trekking and sightseeing in the area.
After breakfast your guide will escort the group on a leisurely walk to Sanje Falls, with a chance to take a refreshing swim in the falls. A picnic lunch will be provided.

▶ Save your work, close all your documents and exit Word!

Exercise

As home-watch coordinator you need to prepare a letter to send to homes in your local area about a special crime awareness initiative.

1. Open the **Elegant Letter** template provided with Microsoft Word and use it to create the following letter. Save the file as **letter.doc**.

JOHN RUDDICK
HOME WATCH CO-ORDINATOR
26 THE GARDENS, DARKSHAM, HANTS TY5 4RF

May 3rd 2003

Mr & Mrs K Hills
The White House
Belevedere Road
Darksham
Hants TY5 23RF

Dear Mr & Mrs Hills

As we enter the holiday season the local police have asked Home Watch co-ordinators to remind local people about the increased risks of burglary. If you are planning a break away this summer please ensure that your home is left secure. A house that presents itself as unoccupied and insecure is far more likely to be targeted than one that is properly secured.

Make it look as though your house is occupied and do not advertise your absence.

Install automated / programmable light switches.

Have a neighbour pop round to clear your letter box or doorstep regularly.

Encourage a neighbour to park on your drive.

Do not advertise that you are going away.

Do cancel all regular deliveries.

Do not announce your departure to a shop-full of people.

Do not have your address showing on your luggage for the outward journey.

Help us to fight local crime and enjoy that holiday!

Yours sincerely

John Ruddick
Home Watch Coordinator
☎ 01543 672345

---

2. Right-align the date and left-align the closing text as shown.

3. Double-line space the list of security measures and insert the telephone symbol as shown.

4. Click on each section of text and count the number of different styles used.

5. Save the document.

6. Copy and paste the list of security measures into a new document and save as **poster.doc**. You will use this at the end of the next chapter.

Tabs, Borders and Lists

Introduction to tabs

In this chapter you will be learning how to make neat lists – such as price lists, lists of travel times, numbered steps in assembling flat-pack furniture, or any other list you can think of.

When you want items to line up neatly in columns, you need to use the **Tab** key. Pressing the **Tab** key will advance the cursor to the next preset Tab stop. In the list below, the first column is left-aligned, the second is centre-aligned, the third is aligned on the decimal point and the last column is right-aligned. This is achieved by setting different tab stops, which appear as marks on the ruler underneath the Formatting toolbar.

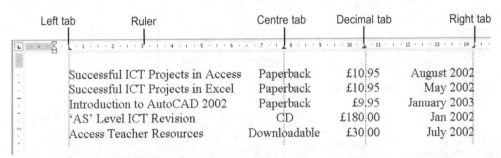

Before you set any tab stops, Microsoft Word has **default tab positions** which appear as faint marks below the ruler.

○ Open a new document and look at the ruler line at the top of the screen. The default tab positions are probably set at intervals of 0.5 inches or 1.27cm.

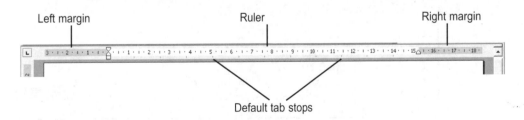

You are going to produce a price list for a company selling stationery items, similar to the one at the bottom of this page.

Setting default tab stops

We will start by changing the default tab positions.

 ◗   Select **Format** from the Main Menu bar. Then click on **Tabs**. A dialogue box like this should appear.

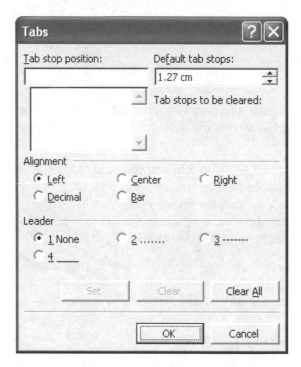

 ◗   Click the up-arrow on the right-hand side of the **Default tab stops** box until it is set at **3cm**. Then click **OK**.

Typing the price list

Type the following list, pressing **Tab** between each entry. You will need to press **Tab** twice after the word **Description**.

ECONOMY SQUARE-CUT FOLDERS			
Product Code	Description	Qty	Price per pack
ESF151	Coloured folders	100	£12.99
ESF152	Buff Folders	50	£4.49
ESF003	Assorted coloured folders	100	£11.99
ESF004	Assorted coloured folders	10	£6.99

You may see a red wavy line under the word **coloured**. This is because Microsoft Word, being an American product, thinks this word is spelt wrongly.

◉ Right-click the word **Coloured**. A pop-up window appears. You can select either **Ignore All**, or **Add to Dictionary**. You will probably have to do this twice, for the capitalised and non-capitalised words.

Tip:

If you are working on a network, you may not be able to add words to the dictionary.

Displaying non-printing characters

Although the list looks quite neat, it would be better if the quantities were right-aligned, and the prices lined up on the decimal point.

Many of the characters that Word stores in your document are 'non-printing' and do not normally show on the screen. These characters include **Tab**, **Enter** and even spaces between words.

Sometimes it is useful to be able to see these characters and you can display them by clicking the **Show/Hide** icon.

◉ Click the **Show/Hide** icon on the Standard toolbar.

Your document now appears like this:

```
ECONOMY·SQUARE-CUT·FOLDERS¶
¶
Product·Code  →  Description  →        →    Qty  →    Price·per·pack¶
ESF151   →    Coloured·folders→    →    100  →    £12.99¶
ESF152   →    Buff·Folders →    →    50   →    £4.49¶
ESF003   →    Assorted·coloured·folders  →   100  →    £11.99¶
ESF004   →    Assorted·coloured·folders  →   10   →    £6.99¶
¶
¶
```

Note:

The different symbols which appear are for a **Space**, **Enter** and **Tab**. Wherever the **Enter** key has been pressed to create a new paragraph, a sign like a backwards P appears, as on the **Show/Hide** icon.

You can see that you have two **Tab** characters in some places, for example between **Description** and **Qty**.

◉ Click **Show/Hide** again to hide the non-printing characters.

Setting custom tabs

We will set our own tab positions.

▶   Select the list and the column headings you have just typed, starting at **Product Code**.

▶   Select **Format** from the Main Menu bar. Then click on **Tabs**.

▶   In the **Tab Stop Position** box, type **3** and then click **Set**.

The next tab position needs to be right-aligned at approximately 9.5cm.

▶   In the **Tab Stop Position** box, type **9.5**. Under **Alignment**, click **Right**. Then click **Set**.

▶   In the **Tab Stop Position** box, type **14.5**. Under **Alignment**, click **Decimal**. Then click **Set**.

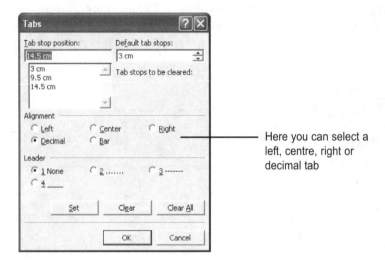

Here you can select a left, centre, right or decimal tab

▶   Click **OK**.

Oh dear! What has gone wrong? The problem is that when you set custom tabs, the default tabs disappear. Remember that you pressed **Tab** twice after **Description**. Now we only have one tab stop where previously there were two.

ECONOMY SQUARE-CUT FOLDERS		
Product Code	Description	Qty
	Price per pack	
ESF151	Coloured folders	100
	£12.99	
ESF152	Buff folders	50
	£4.49	
ESF003	Assorted coloured folders 100	£11.99
ESF004	Assorted coloured folders 10	£6.99

Luckily this is easy to fix. You need to delete the extra **Tab** characters.

- ◗ Click **Show/Hide** again to display the hidden **Tab** characters.
- ◗ Click just before the word **Qty** and press **Backspace**.
- ◗ Click just before **100** on the next line and press **Backspace**.
- ◗ Delete the other superfluous tab on the next line.
- ◗ Hide the **Tab** characters again.

Now everything is looking pretty good except that the prices are too far to the right.

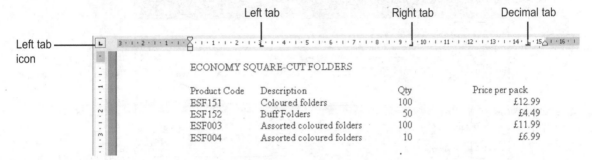

Adjusting tab stops on the ruler

You can change the position of a tab stop by dragging it left or right on the ruler.

- ◗ Highlight the four lines of the list, excluding the column headers.
- ◗ Look at the ruler line and at the far right at position 14.5, note the **Decimal tab icon**.
- ◗ Drag the **Decimal tab icon** to 13.5 on the ruler.

Setting and removing left, centre, right and decimal tabs

At the left of the ruler you will see the tab alignment button.

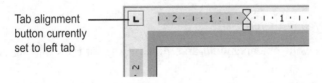

Tab alignment button currently set to left tab

To set a left, centre, right or decimal tab, you click this button repeatedly until the tab type that you want is shown. Then click in the ruler line at the position where you want the tab stop.

| Left tab | Centre tab | Right tab | Decimal tab |

You can delete an unwanted tab stop by dragging it up or down off the ruler.

Adding a border

We can add a border to the list.

◉   Select the whole list and the headings.

◉   From the menu select **Format**, **Borders and Shading**.

◉   Under **Setting**, click the **Box** icon. The other options should be as shown below.

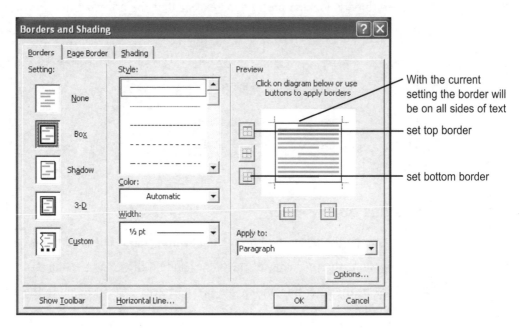

◉   Currently the **Box** border is selected, and the picture on the right-hand side of the window shows that a border will be placed all around the text.

Note that to put a border at the top and/or bottom of the list instead of all around it, you would click the icons as shown in the screenshot above and then click **OK**.

◉   Click **OK**.

A box will appear around the price list.

◉   You can make your headings bold and increase the font size of the main heading.

ECONOMY SQUARE-CUT FOLDERS			
Product Code	**Description**	**Qty**	**Price per pack**
ESF151	Coloured folders	100	£12.99
ESF152	Buff folders	50	£4.49
ESF003	Assorted coloured folders	100	£11.99
ESF004	Assorted coloured folders	10	£6.99

◉   Save your list as **Price List.doc**.

Creating a bulleted list

You are going to create a poster to help with a typical office problem – working the coffee machine.

Using the Coffee Machine

- Put a sheet of paper in the coffee compartment.

- Measure coffee into filter paper – one tablespoon of coffee for each cup you are making.

- Using the scale marked on the side of the jug, fill the jug with the required amount of water.

- Pour the water into the top compartment, and place the jug on the base of the machine.

- Turn the machine on and wait for your coffee to filter through.

Modifying the document setup

When you open a new document the page size, orientation (portrait or landscape) and margins are set to default values. You can change any of these attributes.

◗ Open a new document.

◗ From the **File** menu select **Page Setup**.

The Page Setup window will appear:

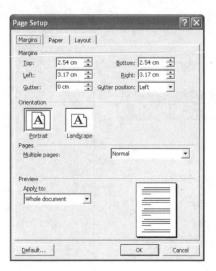

● Click the **Paper** tab.

● Change the **Paper size** to **A5** and then click the **Margins** tab.

● Change the top, bottom, left and right margins to **2cm**. Leave the gutter size as it is, and leave the orientation as **Portrait** rather than **Landscape**. Click **OK**.

● Select a suitable font for the title. The one shown on the previous page is **Albertus Medium**, size **26**.

● Type the heading and make sure that it is **Centred**.

● Press **Enter** twice after the heading and change to a different font. The one shown above is **Arial**, size **14**.

Tip:
Use **Landscape** orientation when you want the page to be wider than it is long.

Making bullets

 ● Click the **Bullets** button on the Formatting toolbar.

● Type the instructions listed in the figure on the previous page. Each time you press **Enter**, a bullet will automatically appear on the next line.

● After typing the last item in the list, press **Enter** once more.

● Turn off the bullets by clicking the **Bullets** button again.

Tip:
You can add bullets after typing a list, rather than before.
Just select the items you want to bullet, and then click the **Bullets** button.

Customising bullets

You can alter the appearance of bullets.

❿   Select the list.

❿   From the **Format** menu select **Bullets and Numbering**.

The following window will appear:

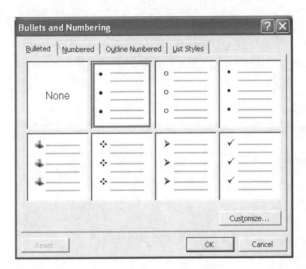

❿   Select a different type of bullet, and click **OK**.

To remove bullets, select the bulleted list and then click the **Bullets** button. This button acts as a 'toggle'.

> **Tip:**
> Further customising options are available if you click the **Customize** button in this window

A numbered list

Instead of using bullets, sometimes you may want to number your steps.

❿   Select the list.

❿   Click the **Numbering** icon on the Formatting toolbar.

Your list will appear with numbers instead of bullets. Note that you can customise numbers in the same way as you customised the bullets. Sometimes you may want a list that uses Roman numerals, or one that has some unnumbered text in the middle of the list. Then you will have to select **Format, Bullets and Numbering** and use the **Customize** options to get the numbering correct.

❿   Click the **Numbering** icon again to remove the numbers.

Leave the list as a bulleted list for the purposes of this exercise.

Spacing paragraphs

Every time you press **Enter**, you create a new paragraph. So, in your list, **Word** treats each separate bullet point as a separate paragraph. You can put extra space between each bullet point so that the list fills the page more neatly.

- If the list is not already selected, select it now.

- Right-click the list to display a shortcut menu.

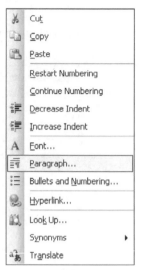

- Select **Paragraph**. The following window appears:

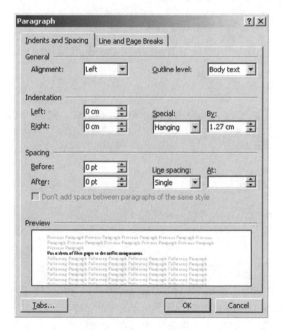

- In the **Spacing Before** box, click the up-arrow until **12** is displayed. Click **OK**.

- If that is not enough spacing to comfortably fill your page, try again. You could try increasing the **Spacing Before** to size **18**, or alternatively you could insert some **Spacing After** each paragraph using the Spacing After box.

- Experiment until you are happy with the layout.

Indenting paragraphs

Notice that in the paragraph dialogue box shown in the figure opposite, under **Indentation** in the box labelled **Special**, **Hanging** appears. What is a hanging indent? It is an indent that is the opposite of a first line left indent. In other words, the first line is not indented but all the subsequent lines in the paragraph are. So in this list, the bullets are not indented but the text is indented by 1.27cm.

If you wanted to change the amount of space between the bullet and the text, you could do it here.

If you are writing a letter or story, you might want to set a **first line** indent, to indent the first line of each paragraph. You would do this by selecting **First line** in the **Special** box.

You can set left and right indents by selecting appropriate options in this dialogue box.

Inserting a soft carriage return

Sometimes you want to have a second paragraph under a bullet point, that does not have its own bullet. You can insert a soft carriage return (line break) by holding down **Shift** and pressing **Enter**.

● Try pressing **Shift** and **Enter** at the end of the first paragraph and inserting the words:

The filter papers are in the drawer under the counter.

 ● Click the **Show/Hide** icon to see what hidden character has been inserted. Click it again to hide the hidden characters.

Placing a border around the page

You can put a border round the whole page.

● On the **Format** menu, select **Borders and Shading**.

 ● Click the **Page Border** tab. Click the **Box** icon and then click **OK**.

Shading the title

We will make the heading yellow on a blue background.

● Select the title by clicking in the left margin next to it.

 ● Click on the arrow next to the **Font Color** button on the Drawing toolbar, and select a colour for your title.

● Now, keeping the heading selected, select **Format** from the Main Menu bar. Then click on **Borders and Shading**.

● Make sure the **Shading** tab is selected.

A dialogue box like the one below will appear:

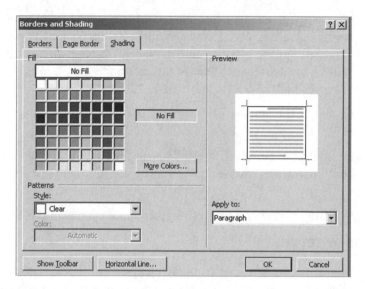

- Choose a shade to go behind your heading, and click **OK**.
- When you are happy with your poster, save and print it.
- Close your document. To do this you can simply click the **Close** icon in the top right-hand corner of the screen.

Automatic hyphenation

If a word is too long to fit on the end of a line, Microsoft Word moves the word to the beginning of the next line instead of hyphenating it. You can turn on automatic hyphenation from the **Tools** menu by selecting **Language**, **Hyphenation** and then selecting **Automatically hyphenate document**.

You can turn automatic hyphenation off using the same dialogue box. Hyphenation is useful to eliminate gaps in justified text or to maintain even line lengths in very narrow columns of text.

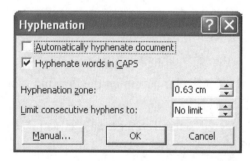

Exercise

This exercise develops the poster that you began at the end of the previous chapter.

1. Open the file **poster.doc.**

2. Insert a heading **Going away on holiday?** in Comic sans MS, size 24, bold.

3. Colour the text and shade the title in colours of your choice.

4. Change the font of the list items to Comic Sans MS, size 16, single line-spaced.

5. Add bullets to the list of security measures. Choose special coloured symbols for the bullets.

6. Insert paragraph spacing of 18pt before each bullet point.

7. Leave a blank line beneath the list and change the font size to 14. Enter the following text:

   For more advice contact Darksham Police station on 01543 587435 or one of your local Home Watch co-ordinators:

8. Leave a blank line and set up custom tab stops at 3.5cm and 11cm. Select leader dots for the second tab stop. Enter the following details:

   Stanley Smith   01543 723433

   Samir Dall   01543 423788

   John Ruddick   01543 672345

9. Insert a decorative border around the page.

10. Save your work.

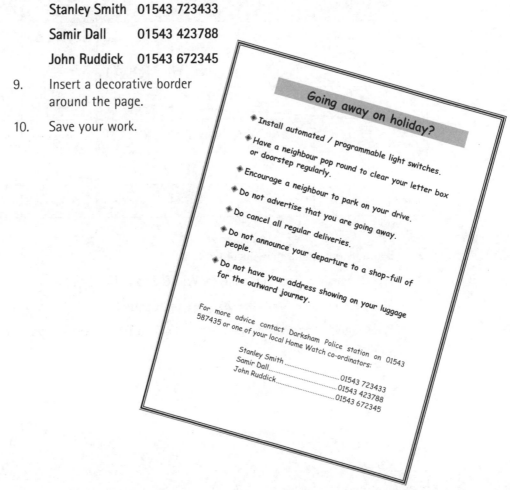

Using Tables

In this chapter, you will learn how to insert a table into a document and type out a timetable or itinerary like the one shown below:

Programme for Winter Sports Holiday

	Monday	Tuesday	Wednesday	Thursday	Friday	Saturday
10-12	Snowboarding	Snowboarding	Beginners Skiing	Snowboarding	Snowboarding	Beginners Skiing
12-2	LUNCH BREAK					
2-4	Beginners Skiing	Tobogganing	Experienced Skiing	Skidoo	Tobogganing	Experienced Skiing
4-6	Experienced Skiing	Skidoo	Ice Skating	Skidoo	Tobogganing	Snowboarding
6-8	DINNER					
8-late	Apres-Ski	Karaoke	Late-night Skiing	Apres-Ski	Ice Skating	Leaving Party

- Begin by opening a new document.

- Type the heading – **Programme for Winter Sports Holiday**.

- Make the heading **Arial**, size **20**, **Bold** and **Centred**.

- Press **Enter** twice and change the font back to **Times New Roman**, size **10**, **left aligned** and not bold.

Inserting a table

○ From the Main Menu bar, select **Table**, **Insert**, **Table**.

You will see a dialogue box like the one below.

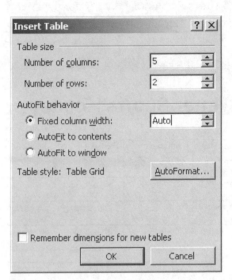

○ Type **7** as the number of columns (or use the arrows).

○ Press the **Tab** key to move to the next box and enter **7**.

○ Leave the **Column width** as **Auto** and click the **OK** button.

A table will be inserted into your document like this:

Programme for Winter Sports Holiday						

○ The cursor should be flashing in the first **cell**, which is in the top left-hand corner of the table.

○ The first cell is going to remain blank. Press **Tab** to move one cell to the right.

○ Type **Monday** and then tab to the next cell.

○ Type **Tuesday**, **Wednesday**, etc in the cells across the top row.

○   Press **Tab** to go to the first cell of the second row.

○   Now fill in the rest of the programme so that it looks like the one below.

Tip:

Once you have typed the first few letters of **Monday**, Word guesses what you are typing and displays **Monday** as a tool tip. You can now just press **Enter** to complete the rest of the word. This will be repeated for the rest of the days that you enter.

Programme for Winter Sports Holiday

	Monday	Tuesday	Wednesday	Thursday	Friday	Saturday
10-12	Snowboarding	Snowboarding	Beginners Skiing	Snowboarding	Snowboarding	Beginners Skiing
12-2	LUNCH BREAK					
2-4	Beginners Skiing	Tobogganing	Experienced Skiing	Skidoo	Tobogganing	Experienced Skiing
4-6	Experienced Skiing	Skidoo	Ice Skating	Skidoo	Tobogganing	Snowboarding
6-8	DINNER					
8-late	Apres-Ski	Karaoke	Late-night Skiing	Apres-Ski	Ice Skating	Leaving Party

Selecting cells

When you want to change the format of one or more cells, for example to change the font or shading, you first have to select the cells to change. Here are some of the ways of selecting cells:

❶   To select the **entire table**, click the cursor in any of the cells in the table. Then from the Main Menu bar select **Table**, **Select**, **Table**. Or, drag across all the cells in the table.

❶   To select a **row**, click next to the row in the left margin. Or, drag across all the cells in the row.

❶   To select a **column**, move the pointer above the column till it turns into a down-arrow, then click. Or, drag across all the cells in the column.

❶   To select a **cell**, from the Main Menu bar select **Table**, **Select**, **Cell**. Or, triple-click in the cell.

Tip:

You can use the **Table**, **Select** menu to select a table, column, row or cell. You may have noticed a small four-pointed arrow in a box over the top left-hand corner of your table. By clicking on it you can select the whole table. This is quicker and more convenient than using the menu.

Modifying row height

The programme looks rather cramped. It would look better if it was more spread out.

○ With the cursor in any of the cells of the table, select **Table** from the Main Menu bar. Then click **Select, Table**. The whole table will be highlighted.

○ Select **Table** again from the Main Menu bar. Then click **Table Properties**.

A dialogue box will appear.

○ Click on the **Row** tab and make entries to match those entered below. The height of each row should be **At least 1cm**.

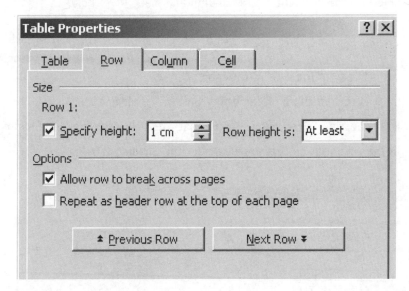

○ Click the **Table** tab. In the Alignment section, click the button for **Center** alignment and then click **OK**. This will centre the table between the left and right margins of the page.

Merging cells in a table

If you look at your programme, you will see that the breaks for lunch and dinner occur at the same time every day. You are able to spread the words **Lunch Break** and **Dinner** across several cells to make your table look more balanced.

○ Drag across the row of cells for the **Lunch Break** period.

○ From the Main Menu bar, select **Table**. Then select **Merge Cells**.

○ Click the **Center** and **Bold** buttons on the Formatting toolbar. You can probably make the font bigger too – say size **18**.

○ Repeat this process for the **Dinner** period of your table.

Formatting text in cells

- ◐   Click in the first cell of the table and drag across and down until you are in the bottom right corner of the table to select the cells.
- ◐   Click the **Center** button on the Formatting toolbar.
- ◐   Click in the left margin beside the top row to select it. Click the **Bold** button on the Formatting toolbar.

You can try out this way of selecting a column – position the cursor just over the top line of the column until it changes to a downward-pointing arrow. Then click.

- ◐   Select all the cells in the first column and make them **Bold**.

Shading

You can shade any of the cells in the table.

- ◐   Click in the left margin beside the top row to select it.
- ◐   From the Main Menu bar, select **Format**. Then click **Borders and Shading**.
- ◐   In the dialogue box that appears, click the **Shading** tab.

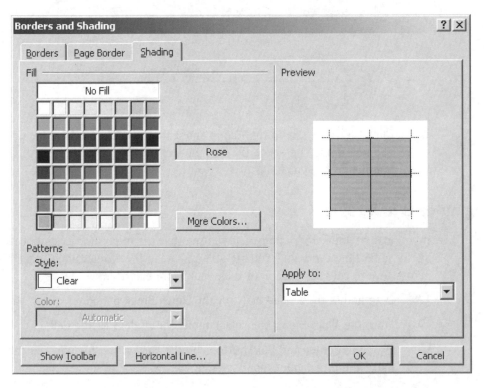

- ◐   Click a colour for the shading and then click **OK**.

	Monday	Tuesday	Wednesday	Thursday	Friday	Saturday
10-12	Snowboarding	Snowboarding	Beginners Skiing	Snowboarding	Snowboarding	Beginners Skiing
12-2	LUNCH BREAK					
2-4	Beginners Skiing	Tobogganing	Experienced Skiing	Skidoo	Tobogganing	Experienced Skiing
4-6	Experienced Skiing	Skidoo	Ice Skating	Skidoo	Tobogganing	Snowboarding
6-8	DINNER					
8-late	Apres-Ski	Karaoke	Late-night Skiing	Apres-Ski	Ice Skating	Leaving Party

Changing cell borders

You can set the borders of any cell, or the whole table, to a specified width and style.

◉ Click anywhere in the table.

◉ From the Main Menu bar, select **Format**. Then click **Borders and Shading**.

◉ In the dialogue box that appears, click the **Borders** tab.

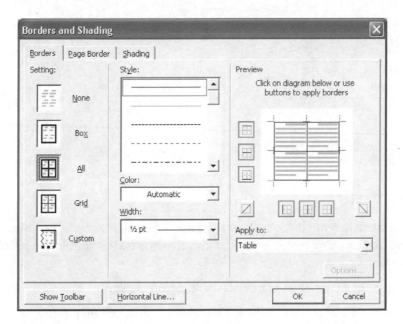

◉ Make sure **Setting** is set to **All**. Scroll down the styles in the Style box to select a different style or leave the style as it is. Change the width to **1pt**. Notice that this border style will **Apply to** the **Table**.

◉ Click **OK**.

Tip:
Notice that you can change the colour of the borders in this dialogue box by clicking the down-arrow in the **Color:** box and selecting a colour.

Inserting and deleting rows and columns

Suppose you wanted to insert an extra row above the row for **2-4**.

○   Click anywhere in the row for **2-4**, then from the Main Menu bar select **Table, Insert, Rows Above**.

○   Delete the row again by selecting **Table, Delete, Rows**.

○   If you want to insert an extra row at the end of a table, click in the very last cell (in the bottom right of the table) and press the **Tab** key. You can delete this row again if you wish.

Columns are inserted and deleted in exactly the same way, by selecting **Column** instead of **Row** from the **Table, Insert** or **Delete** menu.

Changing column widths

To change the width of a column, put the pointer over one of the boundary lines separating the cells. When the pointer changes to a double-headed arrow, you can drag the boundary line either way to make the column wider or narrower.

	Monday
10-12	Snowboarding
12-2	
2-4	Beginners

Centring text vertically

You have already centred the text *horizontally* so that it appears in the middle of the columns. You can also centre it *vertically*, so that the text is right in the middle of the cell.

○   From the Main Menu bar, select **Table, Select, Table**.

○   Right-click anywhere in the table and hover over **Cell Alignment**.

○   Of the nine options given, choose the middle one - **Align Centre**.

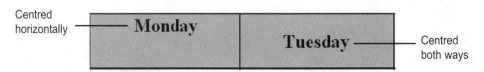

Centred horizontally — Monday   Tuesday — Centred both ways

○   Save your table with a suitable name and view it in Print Preview mode before printing it.

Exercise

You have been asked to produce a programme of events for the annual agricultural show.

1. In a new Word document create a table of 3 columns and 12 rows.

2. Enter the following information:

Barksfield Show 2003		
Day 1 – Wed 28 May		
Time	Event	Venue
9.00am	Judging – Dairy goats	President's ring
	Judging – Flower arranging	Main marquee
10.00am	Horse shoeing competition	Heavy horse ring
	Sheep shearing	Sheep rings
12.30pm	Birds of Prey	President's ring
	Sheepdogs	Sheep rings
3.00pm	Judging – Commercial pigs	Ring 9
	Judging – Rare cattle	Cattle rings
	Vintage tractors	President's ring

3. Make the heading in the first cell Arial size 20, bold and dark green.

4. Merge and centre the cells in the top row.

5. Make the remaining text in the table Arial, size 14. Adjust the column widths to fit.

6. Insert a blank row above each of rows 4, 6, 8 and 10.

7. Insert line spacing of 3pt above each of and 3pt below in all cells.

8. Centre the table on the page.

9. Embolden, merge and shade cells as shown in the finished programme below.

Barksfield Show 2003		
Day 1 – Wed 28 May		
Time	Event	Venue
9.00am	Judging – Dairy goats	President's ring
	Judging – Flower arranging	Main marquee
10.00am	Horse shoeing competition	Heavy horse ring
	Sheep shearing	Sheep rings
12.30pm	Birds of Prey	President's ring
	Sheepdogs	Sheep rings
3.00pm	Judging – Commercial pigs	Ring 9
	Judging – Rare cattle	Cattle rings
	Vintage tractors	President's ring

10. Save the document as **Programme.doc**

Headers, Footers and Graphics

In this chapter we will create a report with a header and footer. We will also import a graphic to insert in the report.

Headers and footers are used to display text that is to appear on every page of a document. A header appears at the top of a page and a footer at the bottom. Either may contain information such as the page number, date, author, file name etc.

For this exercise, there is no need to type an enormous amount of text to illustrate the use of headers and footers. We will just type a heading and one or two sentences on each of two pages.

○ Open a new blank document.

○ Type the following text, using **Heading 1** style for the headings and **Normal** style for the text.

Tip:
Either select the style from the **Style** box before you start typing, or select the text after typing it and apply the style by selecting it from the **Style** box.

Letter from the Chairman
This year marks our fortieth anniversary – a milestone of which we can be proud. The GEA has come a long way since 1962, and the journey has been both challenging and fruitful.

Our work
All GEA's work has a global impact. Although we are best known for our work to protect endangered species, this is merely a part of what we do.

Inserting a header and footer

We will insert a header that contains a date, and a footer that contains the file name on the left and the page number in the middle.

○ From the **View** menu select **Header and Footer**.

A Header and Footer toolbar appears automatically.

Insert Page
Number

Insert
Date

Switch between
Header and Footer

Insert file
location etc.

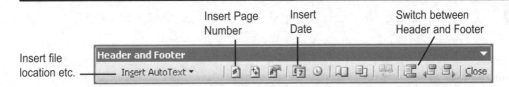

The cursor will be positioned in the Header ready for you to enter something, and the
text in the rest of the document will be greyed out.

◉ Click the **Insert Date** button on the Header and Footer toolbar. Today's date will
be automatically inserted. It may appear in the American format of **mm/dd/yyyy**,
and the easiest way of getting the correct format is to delete it and type the
date in yourself!

◉ Click the **Switch between Header and Footer** button.

◉ In the Footer, press the **Tab** key. Click the **Insert Page Number** button and a **1**
appears.

◉ Now press the **Space** bar, type **of** and press the **Space** bar again. Then find and
click the **Insert Number of Pages** button.

◉ Press **Tab** again and type **Chairman's Report**.

Tip:

There are three set Tab positions in the Header and Footer, for the left, centre
and right-hand side. Pressing **Tab** once moves the cursor to the centre of the
footer.

Your footer should look like this:

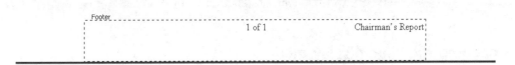

Note that you can enter other items such as the file name and path (i.e the file
location) in the header or footer – if you select **Insert Autotext** you will see the
following list which you can select from:

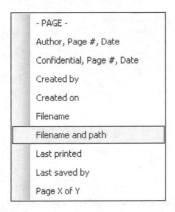

Tip:
If you just want a page number
and nothing else, use **Insert**,
Page Number instead of
inserting a footer.

◗   Click the **Close** button on the Header and Footer toolbar so that you can see the document text.

You can easily modify the text in a header or footer. Double-click the footer and then edit the text so that it **says Chairman's report 2003**. Click the **Close** button in the Header and Footer toolbar. To edit text in the header, double-click the Header.

◗   Save the document as **Chairman's Report**.

Inserting a page break

◗   Now insert a page break before the second paragraph by clicking just before the second heading and holding down **Ctrl** while you press **Enter**.

You can also insert a page break by selecting **Insert**, **Break** from the menu bar, then specifying **Page Break**.

Notice that the footer now says **1 of 2** because you have created a second page.

Using the Zoom tool

You will probably not be able to see the whole page on the screen. You can 'zoom out' using the **Zoom** tool to display the whole page.

◗   Click the down-arrow beside the **Zoom** tool and select **75%**. | 75% ▼ |

If you still cannot see the whole page, try typing **65%** into the box and pressing **Enter**.

> **Note:**
> You can also zoom in to take a closer look at part of a page. This can be useful when you are working with graphics ... or if your eyesight is poor.

Changing the page display mode

It can be useful to view your text in a different layout, especially now it is on two pages.

◗   Click **Normal** from the **View** menu. Now your document will appear like this:

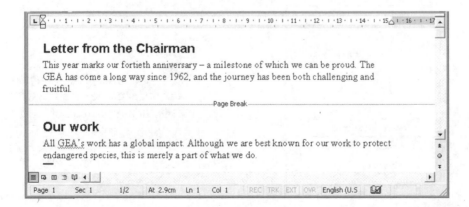

Saving a document for the Web

You can also select **Web Layout** view, to see what the page would look like if it was posted on a web site.

- ○ Click **Web Layout** from the **View** menu.

You can save a document in a format suitable for saving to the Web.

- ○ From the File menu select **Save As**.

- ○ In the **Save As Type** box, click the down-arrow and select **Web Page (*.htm; *.html)**

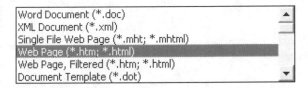

- ○ Click **Cancel** for now because we are not going to post this page to a web site.

- ○ Return to **Print Layout** view by selecting it from the **View** menu.

- ○ Save your document as **ChairmansReport.doc**.

Importing graphics

We will import a graphics file to put in the report. The graphics file is called **fishcage.jpg** and can be downloaded into your computer from our web site **www.payne-gallway.co.uk**. To do this, click **Resources** on the Home page and select **Student**. From then on it will be self-explanatory.

First of all, add a bit more text to the end of your document.

- ○ Type the following text, using style **Heading 3** for the heading and **Normal** for the rest of the text:

Marine Conservation

The goal of our marine programme is to improve nature conservation, resource management and pollution prevention. We work with people whose livelihoods depend on the seas to secure the long-term health of marine ecosystems.

- ○ Make sure you have pressed **Enter** at the end of the text so that the cursor is on a new line. Press **Enter** again to leave a blank line.

 ▶ From the **Insert** menu select **Picture, From File**.

 ▶ Find the picture **fishcage.jpg** which you downloaded.

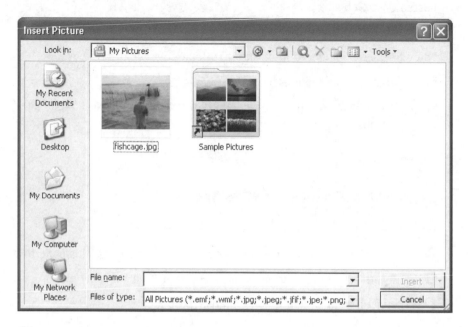

 ▶ Click **Insert**.

The graphic will now appear underneath the text.

 ▶ Click the graphic to select it. Black handles will appear around it.

Re-sizing an image

Once a graphic is selected you can drag any of the corner handles to make it bigger or smaller. If you drag one of the handles in the middle of a side you will change the proportions of the picture and it will appear distorted.

○ Drag the bottom right-hand handle (which is hard to see against the background of the sea) upwards and inwards to make the picture about half the size. The pointer changes to a diagonal double-headed arrow when you click and hold over a corner handle.

○ Centre the picture while it is still selected by clicking the **Centre** button on the Formatting toolbar.

Moving an image

When a selected graphic has black handles around it, it is embedded in the text and cannot be moved about except by positioning it to the left, right or centre as you can with text.

If you want to move it, you must change the **wrapping style**.

○ With the graphic selected, select **Format Picture** from the menu bar.

Tip:
You can also use a shortcut: Right-click the picture and select **Format Picture**.

○ The Format Picture window appears. Click the tab labelled **Layout**.

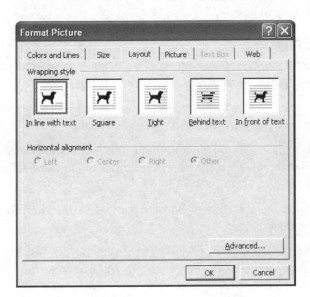

○ Click the **Tight** layout and click **OK**.

The image should now have white handles around it and you can drag it up into the text.

○ Position the graphic to the right of the text. Size it if necessary.

Our work

All GEA's work has a global impact. Although we are best known for our work to protect endangered species, this is merely a part of what we do.

Marine Conservation

The goal of our marine programme is to improve nature conservation, resource management and pollution prevention. We work with people whose livelihoods depend on the seas to secure the long-term health of marine ecosystems.

Copying or deleting an image

Once the image is selected, you can delete it simply by pressing the **Delete** key. You can also cut or copy it onto the clipboard and then paste it to another part of your document, or into another document.

- ◗   Try copying the graphic to the first page of the document by clicking the **Copy** button while the graphic is selected. Move to the first page and click the **Paste** button.

- ◗   Undo the Paste, as you do not need two copies of the image.

- ◗   Save and close the document.

Inserting and manipulating charts

Charts created in **MS Excel** can be inserted into a Word document and moved, resized, copied, or deleted in exactly the same way as a picture or image.

In this exercise you will insert a chart from a spreadsheet called Birdschart.xls. You can download this from the web site **www.payne-gallway.co.uk/ecdl**.

- ◗   Open a new document in Word. Type a heading, **This chart shows how English songbirds are under threat**. Change the style of the heading to **Heading 1** style. Press **Enter**.

- ◗   Open Excel and open the spreadsheet **Birdschart.xls**. Click the chart to select it and then click the **Copy** button.

- ◗   Return to your Word document by clicking its title icon in the **Task bar** at the bottom of the screen, and click the **Paste** button. You have now duplicated the chart between a spreadsheet and a document. (you would use exactly the same technique to copy a chart, picture or image to another open document).

- ◗   With the chart still selected, drag a corner handle until it fits neatly under the report heading.

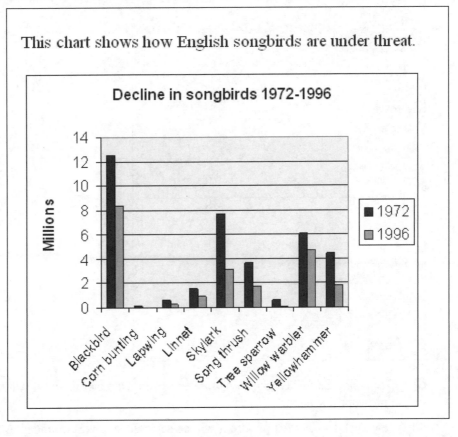

This chart shows how English songbirds are under threat.

Decline in songbirds 1972-1996

Note that when the chart is selected, it has black handles. To move it, you must change the wrapping style exactly as you did when moving an image. When it has white handles you will be able to drag it wherever you want it.

To delete that chart, you would simply select it and press the **Delete** key.

Inserting and manipulating a Clip Art picture in a document

Occasionally you may want to brighten up a document by inserting some Clip Art. MS Office has a collection of Clip Art pictures which you can use in your documents, and you can also purchase Clip Art collections on CD or borrow them from the local library.

You can try inserting a picture of a bird underneath the chart.

- ◗ Double-click underneath the chart to create an insertion point.

- ◗ From the **Insert** menu select **Picture**, **Clip Art**.

- ◗ A **Clip Art** pane appears and you can type a word into the Search box to say what you are looking for.

○ Try typing **Bird**. Then click a picture that is not too awful, and it will be inserted into your document.

When you click the Clip Art picture it will be selected, and is surrounded by black handles.

Note:

❶ To resize the picture, drag a corner handle.

❶ To move the picture, use the same procedure as for an image, already described on Page 3-67.

❶ To copy the picture to another location in the same document, click to select it, then click the **Copy** button. Click where you want to copy it to and click the **Paste** button.

❶ To copy the picture (or an image or chart) into another document, or into your spreadsheet, click to select it, then click the **Copy** button. Restore the spreadsheet by clicking its Title icon in the Task bar, click where you want the picture to appear and click the **Paste** button.

❶ To delete a picture, image or chart, select it and press the **Delete** key.

Using the Help system

If you want to perform a particular function and are uncertain how to do it, you can always try the online Help system.

The **Office Assistant** takes the form of a paperclip, cat, dog or a number of other options.

◗   If the Office Assistant is not already visible on your screen, click **Help** on the menu bar and select **Show the Office Assistant**.

As an example, suppose you need to insert a page break and cannot remember how to do this. The Office Assistant can tell you how to do this.

◗   Click the Office Assistant cartoon.

Tip:

To change the appearance of the Office Assistant, right-click it and select **Choose Assistant**.

◗   Type in **Start a new page**.

⊙   From the new list, select **Insert a manual page break**.

Instructions are displayed:

Insert a manual page break

1. Click where you want to start a new page.
2. On the **Insert** menu, click **Break**.
3. Click **Page break**.

Deleting a page break

⊙   Now see if you can use the Help system to find out how to delete a manual page break. Try clicking the Office Assistant and typing into the box **Delete a page break**.

It may come up with a selection which includes **Troubleshoot page breaks**. If so, select this. It will recommend that you switch to Normal view, select the page break and then press **Delete**.

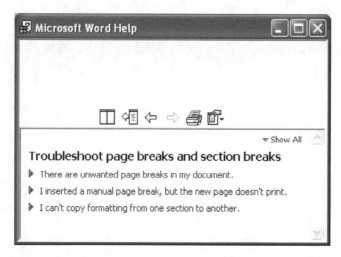

⊙   On the main menu, click **View**, **Normal**.

Tip:
Note that the image does not appear in Normal view!

⊙   Click on the line saying **Page Break** and then press the **Delete** key.

⊙   You can close the **Help** window if it is still open by clicking the **X** in its top right-hand corner.

⊙   Return to **Print Layout** view.

⊙   Save your document and click the **Print Preview** button to view it in Print Preview mode.

Exercise

In this exercise you will develop the programme for the local agricultural show (that you began at the end of the end of the last chapter) into a multi-page document.

1.   Open the file **Programme.doc**.

2.   Insert a page break before the table. On this first page enter a large heading **Barksfield Show 2003 Programme of events**. Enter a sub-heading in a smaller font **Organised by Barksfield Town Council**.

3.   Insert an appropriate piece of Clip Art onto this front cover.

4.   Add a decorative border to this page.

5.   Copy the table (now on page 2) and paste it onto pages 3 and 4 of the document.

6.   Edit the contents of the table on the two new pages to show events taking place on days 2 and 3 of the show.

7.   Insert a footer (on all pages except page 1) that displays the page number in the centre and the text **Barksfield Show 2003** on the right.

8.   Save the document as **Complete Programme.doc** and print.

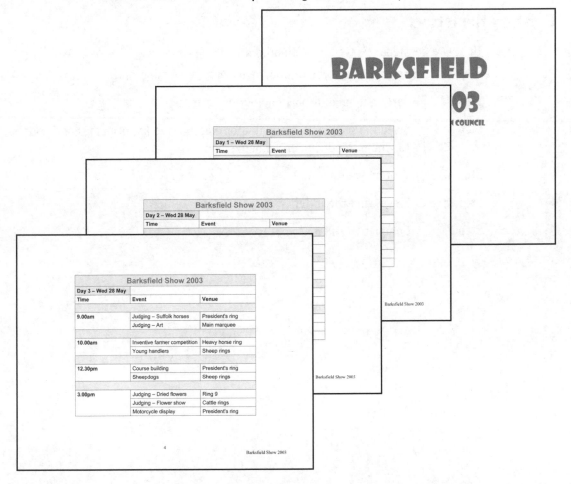

Mail Merge

The mail merge facility is very useful when you want to send the same letter to a number of different people. You can personalise each letter by inserting the correct name, address and other details from a database or other data file.

In this chapter you will edit the letter that you created in Chapter 3.1 and prepare a personalised version to send out to several recipients, and also create address labels for the envelopes.

Creating the letters

There are six steps involved in setting up a mail merge:

Step 1:   Selecting the type of document you are working on.

Step 2:   Setting up and displaying your document.

Step 3:   Selecting recipients – opening or creating the list of names and addresses to whom the document is being sent.

Step 4:   Writing your letter.

Step 5:   Previewing the letters.

Step 6:   Completing the merge.

Step 1:   Selecting the type of document you are working on.

◉ Open the letter you created in Chapter 3.1 – it should be saved as **TanzaniaLetter.doc**.

◉ From the Main Menu bar, select **Tools**, **Letters and Mailings**, **Mail Merge** (**Mail Merge Wizard** in Office XP). The Mail Merge Task pane should appear on the right of the screen.

◉ Make sure you have selected **Letters** as the document type you are working with.

◉ Now click on **Next: Starting document** at the bottom of the Task pane. This will take you on to Step 2.

Step 2:   Select starting document – setting up your letter

◉ You already have the letter open that you want to work on. So select **Use the current document**.

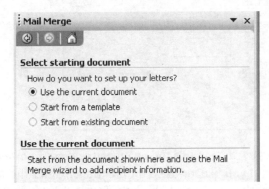

◉ Click on **Next: Select recipients** to move on to Step 3.

Step 3: Selecting recipients

You now have the choice of using an existing data file such as a database table or a spreadsheet, or creating a new list. If you select **Use an existing list**, you will be able to browse through the files on your computer until you find the file you want to use. The data will appear in a **Mail Merge Recipients** box exactly as described near the end of Step 3.

○ You don't currently have any lists or contacts, so you need to create your own. Select the **Type a new list** option and click on **Create** in the section that appears. A dialogue box like the one below should appear.

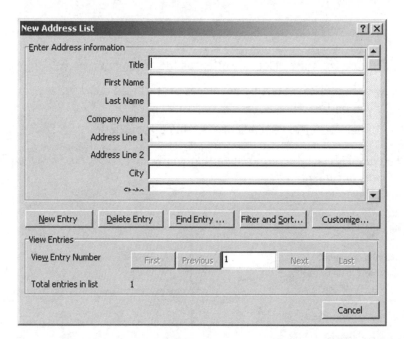

○ Enter a name and address. (You can use the name and address from the letter that you have on-screen if you like, or use a different one.) Enter the post code of the address in the box that is entitled **ZIP Code**. This is simply the American equivalent of our post code.

Tip:
You can press the **Tab** key to move from one box to the next.

You will have left a lot of the boxes in the dialogue box blank – for example **Company name** and **State**. You can delete these unneeded boxes from your records.

○ Click the **Customize** button in the dialogue box. A further dialogue box will appear.

○ Click on the first field name that you don't need – **Company Name**. With this selected, click on the **Delete** button, then click **Yes** to confirm. Repeat this for the other field names that you don't need for your address list. Click **OK**.

○ Now you are back in the **New Address List** box. Click on **New Entry** and the boxes will clear. Don't worry about your first entry – it is automatically saved for you. You can now enter the name and address of a second person to whom you want to send the letter.

○ Fill in the details for your second person and click **New Entry**. Repeat this until you have entered 5 or 6 addresses for your list and then click **Close**. Another dialogue box will appear:

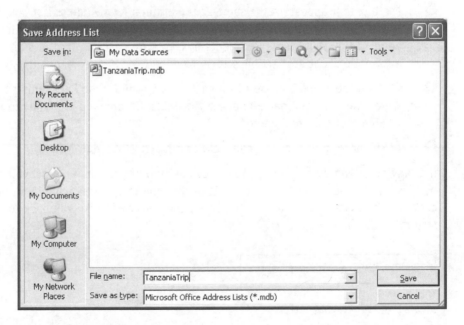

Your address list will automatically be saved as an **.mdb** database file in the **My Data Sources** area of your computer.

○ Save your address list as **TanzaniaTrip.mdb**.

When you have saved your address list, a further box will appear – the **Mail Merge Recipients** box. This allows you to view your completed list of names and addresses and make any amendments – for example you may want to arrange them in a particular order, or perhaps change one of the addresses.

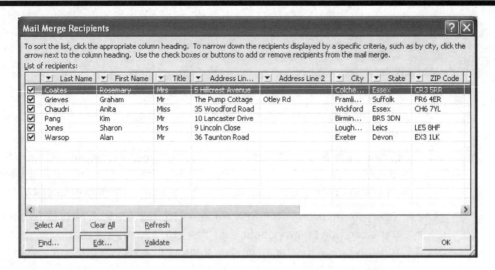

Suppose in the example above you wanted to change **Grieves** to **Greaves**.

○ Select the whole entry by clicking anywhere along the line that contains his information. Then click on the **Edit** button.

○ The box that appears is the same as the original **New Address List** box, except it is now full of the information you stored in it. By selecting Graham Grieves's name in the Mail Merge Recipients box, you are ensuring that it is his information that appears on-screen. Now edit the name, changing it to **Greaves**.

○ Click on **Close** and you are taken back to the Mail Merge Recipients box, in which the amended name appears. Now click **OK** and you are ready to move on to Step 4 of your mail merge.

○ At the bottom of the Task pane, click on **Next: Write your letter**.

If at any point you wish to return to a previous step of your mail merge, you can do so by clicking the back arrow in the top left of the mail merge Task pane. Alternatively, click on **Previous** at the bottom of the Task pane and it will take you back to the last step that you completed.

Step 4: Write your letter

You have already written your letter. However, you do want to add recipient information, in the form of the names and addresses you saved in the previous step. Also, you want to add a greeting line so that all of your letters don't say **Dear Mrs Coates** like the original letter.

○ In your original letter, highlight the name and address you entered beginning **Mrs R. Coates** and ending with the postcode.

○ Now click on **Address Block** in the Task pane. A dialogue box will appear:

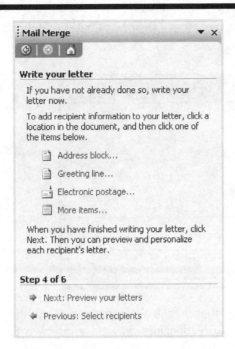

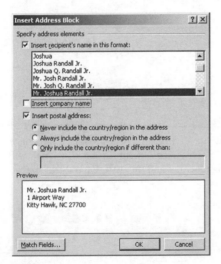

● Choose a suitable format for the recipient's name and set the other options as above. Click **OK**.

● With the insertion point positioned after **««AddressBlock»»**, press **Enter** to create a blank line.

You can carry out many of these tasks using the **Mail Merge** toolbar, which does appear automatically above your main page when carrying out a mail merge. However, it is much easier if you follow the steps through using the **Mail Merge Wizard**, as we have been doing in this chapter.

○ Now highlight the first line of the letter – **Dear Mrs Coates** – and click on **Greeting line** in the Task pane.

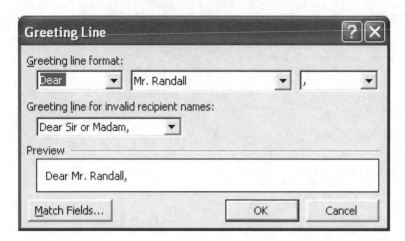

○ Select the Greeting line format that uses just the first name, and then click **OK**. With the insertion point after **«GreetingLine»»** in your letter, press **Enter**.

The screen should now be looking something like this:

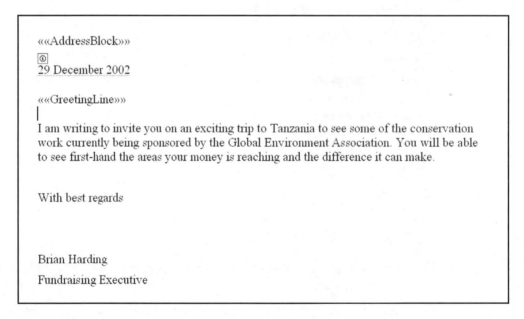

With your letter completed, you are now able to preview and personalise each recipient's letter.

○ Click **Next: Preview your letters** at the bottom of the Task pane.

Step 5: Previewing your letters

○ You should see the preview of the first of your letters, with the address block and the greeting line inserted as you selected. Click on the arrow button to the right of **Recipient: 1** to preview the other letters.

In the address block for each letter, the post code appears on the same line as the city. You may want to change this to ensure that the post code appears on a line of its own - you will be doing this during the final step of the merge.

○ Click **Next: Complete the merge** to move on to the last step of your merge.

Step 6: Completing the merge

You are now ready to complete the merge and produce your letters. However, first you must edit your individual letters to ensure that the post codes are properly positioned in the text.

○ Click on **Edit individual letters**.

○ In the **Merge to New Document** dialogue box select **All** and click **OK**.

○ A new document automatically opens containing all your letters. This document will be called **Letters1**, and you can now scroll down through each letter individually.

◐ In your first letter, press **Enter** immediately before the post code to send it to a new line. Repeat this for the other letters, before saving the file and finally printing. You have now completed your mail merge. The letters can be printed.

Creating mailing labels

You can now create the labels to stick on the envelopes. For this, you can use the same name and address data that you have already stored as **TanzaniaTrip.mdb** and choose to create labels instead of Form letters.

◐ Click the **New Blank Document** button on the Standard toolbar.

◐ From the Main Menu bar, select **Tools, Letters and Mailings, Mail Merge**. The Mail Merge Task pane again appears.

◐ Select the **Labels** option before clicking on **Next: Starting document**.

◐ With **Change document layout** selected, click on **Label options** to choose the size of your labels.

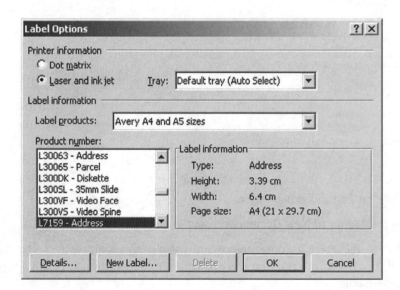

Tip:
If you want a specific type of label that does not appear as an option in the dialogue box, you can create your own custom labels by clicking on **New Label** and entering your own specifications.

○ Select your own size of label from the options shown and click **OK**. A grid of label outlines will appear in your document.

○ Click on **Next: Select recipients** at the bottom of the Task pane.

○ You want to use the same list of data that you used previously in setting up your mail merge. With **Use an existing list** selected, click on **Browse**.

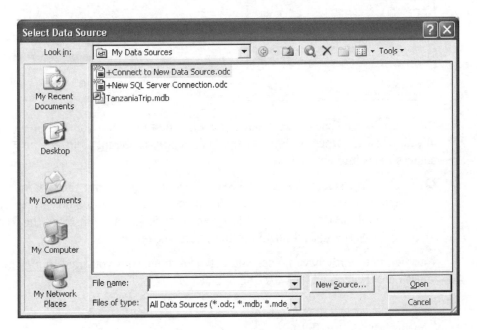

○ In the dialogue box, select the file **TanzaniaTrip.mdb** that you created earlier in the chapter and click **Open**. The Mail Merge Recipients box will open showing the information you saved earlier – simply click **OK**.

○ With the insertion point in the first box in your grid, you are ready to begin putting your data onto the labels. Click on **Next: Arrange your labels** at the bottom of the Task pane.

When performing the actual mail merge, you inserted an **Address block** into your letter. However, you then had to edit the address block because it automatically positioned the post code on the same line as the city. This time you are going to insert the data fields manually.

○ Click on the **More items** option.

The dialogue box below will appear:

The **Insert Merge Fields** box presents you with the fields that you had previously saved in your database when performing the mail merge. You want to insert the name and address fields into your labels.

◉ With **Title** selected, click on **Insert** to insert the field into the first label. Select and insert every other field up to **ZIP code** in the dialogue box. When you have inserted ZIP Code, click on **Close** (which once you have inserted the first field replaces the **Cancel** button in the figure above).

Your fields currently have no spacing between them, so if you tried to preview your labels now they would look like the one below.

MrsRosemaryCoates5 Hillcrest
AvenueColchesterEssexCR3 5RR

◉ Insert a space between «**Title**» and «**First_Name**» by placing the insertion point directly after «**Title**» and pressing the Space bar. Repeat this to insert a space between «**First_Name**» and «**Last_Name**».

◉ Insert a line break after «**Last_Name**» by placing the insertion point directly after it and pressing **Enter**. Repeat this to insert line breaks at the end of every other field in your label apart from the last line of the address, the post code.

◉ Once you have arranged your data fields into the right format, click on the **Update all labels** button to ensure that all of your labels have the same format.

Update all labels

○ Now you are ready to preview your labels – click on **Next: Preview your labels** at the bottom of the Task pane. They should look like this, although you may only see one label at this stage.

Mr Alan Warsop 36 Taunton Road Exeter Devon EX3 1LK	Mrs Sharon Jones 9 Lincoln Close Loughborough Leics LE5 8HF	Mr Kim Pang 10 Lancaster Drive Birmingham BR5 3DN
Miss Anita Chaudri 35 Woodford Road Wickford Essex CH6 7YL	Mr Graham Greaves The Pump Cottage Otley Rd Framlingham Suffolk FR6 4ER	Mrs Rosemary Coates 5 Hillcrest Avenue Colchester Essex CR3 5RR

○ Click on **Next: Complete the merge** to go to the final stage of creating your labels.

○ In the final Task pane, click on **Edit individual labels**. In the **Merge to new document** dialogue box that appears, make sure **All** is selected before clicking **OK**. This creates a new document containing your actual labels with the names and addresses on, probably called **Labels2.doc**. You are now able to make any changes you think need making before saving the labels.

○ Save your labels as **TanzaniaLabels.doc**. If you want to print labels, you should make sure that you have the correct label stationery loaded in the printer.

○ You can save the document which contains the label format as **Labels.doc**.

○ Close both documents.

Exercise

In this exercise you will create a list of names and addresses to receive the letter created at the end of Chapter 3.4. You will use the letter produced at the end of that chapter to perform a mail merge.

1. Open the file **letter.doc**.

2. Delete the addressee details.

3. Use this letter as your starting document in the mail merge.

4. Enter a new list of six contacts that are to receive the letter.

5. Produce the merged letters.

6. Create mailing labels for the envelopes.

7. Save and close your work.